LOOKING FOR FLAVOUR

WAKEFIELD PRESS

BARBARA SANTICH

LOOKING FOR FLAVOUR

Wakefield
Press

Wakefield Press

Box 2266

Kent Town

South Australia 5071

First published 1996

Designed by Liz Nicholson, Design BITE

Illustrations by Danny Snell

Typeset by Clinton Ellicott, MoBros, Adelaide

Printed and bound by Hyde Park Press, Adelaide

National Library of Australia

Cataloguing-in-publication entry

Santich, Barbara.

Looking for flavour.

Bibliography.

ISBN 1 86254 395 X. (Hardcover)

ISBN 1 86254 385 2. (Paperback)

1. Food habits – Australia – History. 2. Food – History.

3. Cookery, Australian – History. I. Title.

641.30994

Promotion of this book was assisted by the
South Australian government through the
Department for the Arts and Cultural Development.

FOR A.E.D.

CONTENTS

FOREWORD

IF YOU ARE INTERESTED in what you eat but only read the pages devoted to food in daily newspapers and glossy magazines you could be forgiven for believing that the newest restaurant and the most currently fashionable produce represent the sum of your stomach's longings. Journalism of this kind, with the odd exception, hardly even touches the sides of the curious and thinking eater. By default, the real concerns of gastronomy are deemed to have no place in accessible publications.

Barbara Santich addresses these concerns. Her essays examine what we eat with all the skills of academic research enlivened by an engaged palate. Nearly two hundred years after Brillat-Savarin published his own meditations on gastronomy, her writings, dependent on the senses and the intellect, continue in the spirit of the mayor of Belley.

Usually and unjustly known for his aphorism: 'Tell me what you eat; I will tell you who you are', Brillat-Savarin defined gastronomy as 'the reasoned understanding of everything that concerns us insofar as we sustain ourselves'. This is Barbara's translation, and she applies this understanding through her emphasis on flavour and her respect for the reconciliation of indulgence with moderation. Elsewhere Barbara has written extensively on the *ménage à trois* (her delicious term) of gastronomy, food and medicine.

Barbara Santich's passionate interest in the here and now shines through in her crusade for markets in our cities and suburbs, in her enquiries into ideas of cuisine and regionalism in Australia, and in recording the ideas eaten at some extraordinary meals that have been part of the series of Symposiums of Australian Gastronomy.

These Symposiums have played a pivotal role in providing reasons for Barbara Santich to write the kind of essay she gives us in this book. And for the past five years, the *Sydney Review* has provided Barbara with the space for a column through which her assertion that 'gastronomy lies at the confluence of the streams of sensuality and intellect' has become manifest to its followers.

Writing about what sustains us, Barbara proclaims the essential subjectivity of the senses – her own gastronomic awakening is unashamedly centred in France. At the same time, with indefatigable research, she uses her intellect to make sense of the table. Our indebtedness to the civilizing pleasures of any table must include a responsibility towards what sits on it and how it arrived there, and making sense of it all. *Looking for Flavour* repays some of that debt.

Gay Bilson

Sydney, 1996

x

'When you wake up in the morning, Pooh,' said Piglet at last,
'what's the first thing you say to yourself?'
'What's for breakfast?' said Pooh. 'What do you say, Piglet?'
'I say, I wonder what's going to happen exciting today?' said Piglet.
Pooh nodded thoughtfully.
'It's the same thing,' he said.

A.A.MILNE, WINNIE-THE-POOH

LOOKING FOR FLAVOUR

What's the smell of parsley? – Dylan Thomas

I DIDN'T THINK SO at the time, but I recognise now that in the environmentally sensitive 1990s the title I had chosen for one of my articles was highly provocative: 'Flavour first, rainforests second'.

Reflecting on it later, I realised that if there has been one constant in all my years of writing around and about food, it's been the importance of flavour. Not just any flavour, but authentic flavour, the flavour of things tasting as I they should – or as I remember them tasting. The flavour of oysters straight from the sea ... as I can still taste them, when my grandfather carved them from the rocks at Sydney's Palm

•

1

•

Beach, washed them in the brine and introduced his four year-old grand-daughter to a flavour she will never forget ... these were the essential oysters.

Years later, in Spain, I wrote about tomatoes. After a morning on the beach, when the others had all retired for their siesta, I would sit on the balcony with a glass of Tarragona wine and fresh crusty bread heavy with olive oil and thick crimson slices of tomato. Looking towards the invisible sea, beyond the railway line and the biscuit-coloured boxes of the new suburbia, I read, and wrote, and relished my solitude as I relished my tomatoes. Those Spanish tomatoes, which we bought every second morning from a farm on the rural outskirts, ten minutes walk away, became imbued with the pleasure and joy of an hour all to myself, and the memory of their flavour is suffused with a feeling of deep contentment. They became the essential tomatoes.

Not every food has its benchmark in my imagination, but the essential chocolate is there, and it comes from the Paris shop of Christian Constant, on the Left Bank, rue du Bac. One Sunday morning, on the way to visit a friend for lunch, we passed by his shop, and left with a selection of the most exquisite, intense and refined chocolate petits fours I have ever experienced. For sharing, we cut each diminutive cube into quarters, but so complex and subtle were these gâteaux that a quarter was more than enough. I revisit the shop every time I am in Paris, just to remember them – and though Christian Constant chocolates have never been quite the same since, the souvenir remains as the yardstick against which all other chocolate may be judged.

Because flavour is important to me I cultivate a summer garden. Perhaps 'cultivate' is too flattering a description for a higgledy-piggledy backyard that has beans mixed up with tomatoes and melons threat-ening to strangle the clothes line, but it's enough to keep me in fresh produce throughout the summer. In spring, it yields sweet, young radishes that demand nothing more, and nothing less, than fresh crusty bread, good butter, and proper salt, and in all seasons it offers fresh herbs for flavouring an omelette, a salad, a dish of potatoes. I haven't always cultivated a garden, but wherever I've lived I've left a legacy of herbs: mint at Jean-Pierre's, its North African ancestors brought to France by itinerant farm workers; tarragon, the soft and delicate true French tarragon, outside the kitchen window near Compiègne; and ineradicable comfrey in the tiny backyard in inner-city Lilyfield. It's not that I like gardening – better to think of it as exer-cise, less enjoyable than sex but infinitely more satisfying than jogging – but its rewards, anticipated and enjoyed, make the effort worthwhile. When I can wander by the garden and check the slowly ripening tomatoes, crush some thyme between my fingers and inhale its uplifting aroma, or crunch on a tiny bean, then I know a garden is a wondrous thing.

Both at the instant and in retrospect, flavour is a distinct but integral part of the eating experience. Sometimes it represents the whole experience, as if taste had dominated the other senses. At other times, though the necessary props are called up, the flavour remains elusive. Try as I may, I can never make my palate recall the taste of my first Bresse chicken, the paragon of flavour in the poultry world. I can remember buying the chicken at the Saturday market in Beaune, in the square next to the wood-and-plaster structure of the centuries-old covered market. It came from a stall next to the second-hand books stall, where I found, and excitedly bought, a long-coveted 1922 two-volume edition of the *Larousse Universel* illustrated dictionary for the bargain price of 100 francs. I don't remember what the chicken cost, but I know that it was a big bird, as chickens go, and that its neck was still covered with white feathers, which, together with its blue legs and authenticating red label, patriotically assured me that this was a genuine *poulet de Bresse*. I remember cooking the bird with loads of my best butter and perhaps a sprig of the tarragon that was just shooting outside the kitchen window, and seeking out one of our better Bordeaux to drink with it. And I remember the firmness of the flesh as I carved it, and how white it was. But its flavour, the essence of that *poulet de Bresse*, eludes me.

Scientists might resolve flavour into its separate components by gas chromatography or other sophisticated techniques and, subsequently, attempt to recreate flavour in the laboratory by working backwards from the results of these analyses and putting together a blend of the identified chemical compounds in the appropriate proportions. Such syntheses never work. The blend is never the same as nature's original. I disliked banana Paddle Pops as a child, and later at university I learnt why: banana was one of the first (and easiest?) flavours to be identified and subsequently synthesised. Convinced that flavour has to be more than chemical formulas, I viewed this advance in chemistry with great scepticism.

Flavour is an evocation, epitomising whole experiences. Particular flavours are associated with particular settings, people, and moods. Looking for flavour is, unconsciously, a personal quest. Certain flavours come to mean friendship, or contentment, or comfort. Chocolate might represent the soothing luxury of self-indulgence; a lemon-sharpened cup of tea the satisfaction of a job well done.

●

●

I cannot think of any flavours I associate with anguish, or anger, or dis-appointment; perhaps these have been selectively culled, or perhaps they never made it to the memory bank in the first place.

The flavour fanatic Dr Max Lake has developed a theory to explain all this. Primitive animals, such as the earthworm, began with simply a 'taste brain' that responded to chemical sensations – the five basic tastes of sweet, sour, salty, bitter and umami (a savoury quality represented by MSG). Later came the 'smell brain', which reached its greatest development in the koala, one of the most particular of animals in its choice of food. We still possess a rudimentary 'taste brain' and 'smell brain', though these are overshadowed by the intelligent brain. The 'smell brain' complex includes a component known as the hippocampus which, amongst other things, preserves our past; Max Lake calls it 'the library of long memory'. This elegantly complex organ serves as a logical base to the magical power of flavour and smell – aromas that construct whole cities, tastes that call up friends as effectively as Aladdin's magic lamp. It's the hippocampus, sparked by messages from a sip of lime tea and a crumb of madeleine, that started Proust on his nostalgic reverie. Further, the integration of the 'smell brain' with various other parts of the cerebral system means the involvement of emotions, so that a particular aroma or flavour might influence the way we feel. Reciprocally, our emotional state also has a bearing on how we taste; absorbed in the monochromatic underworld of self-pity, we lose all sense of smell and flavour.

Half of flavour is aroma, and smells, according to Max Lake, are absolutely fundamental to life. Food smells provoke appetite and help ensure survival of the individual; our own body smells (pheromones) provoke sexual attraction and help ensure survival of the species.

•

5

•

Aromas can serve as a warning to animals, toxic compounds effectively saying 'Avoid me'; they also deliver a cautionary message in my kitchen when they let me know that my beautifully golden apricot jam is starting to catch on the bottom! (The single greatest obstacle to acceptance of the microwave is its indifference to the senses.)

Whenever we smell something, the sensation passes through the olfactory nerves to the 'smell brain', or olfactory cortex, which includes those parts of the brain containing the highest concentrations of beta endorphin. Beta endorphin is also known as the 'happy hormone', since it promotes feelings of pleasure and contentment. It's understandable, then, that the ultimate in flavour experience, whether the 'essential' oyster, or tomato, or chocolate, will bring about a generous endorphin response. And since the endorphins are natural opiates, any other oyster, or tomato, or chocolate, with less of a flavour hit, cannot hope to evoke the same degree of satisfaction and contentment.

Because you know and enjoy the 'high' of the authentic flavour, you keep looking for that 'high', and perhaps the circumstances that surround it: the holiday mood that accompanies the small, sweet school prawns fresh from the lakes, or lazy summers of sun-blessed apricots from a backyard tree. And you are less likely to accept a product of inferior flavour – or only in the full knowledge that it will be less gratifying. When you appreciate the zing of proper coffee, you buy freshly roasted beans and grind them yourself, because as soon as it is ground, even stored airtight, coffee loses the intensity that is part of the 'essential' experience. You know, if you make coffee at home, that its flavour quality also depends on the water (rain water is preferable to Adelaide tap water), on the material of the coffee pot (glass is preferable to plastic), and you will probably think twice about coffee that has been kept warm or, worse, reheated. If you are extremely particular, you will know that coffee tastes better from fine china than thick pottery or plastic. But we all make compromises and desperate times call for desperate measures. Camping rough in Greece and Italy, I put convenience first and accepted instant Nescafé. Not so the Greek and Italian women, who had packed their coffee-making devices with the beach umbrellas and plastic sandals, and who shamed me by serving proper, aromatic coffee every morning.

Max Lake says we all have the equipment that allows us to smell and taste and intellectually process the sensations, but few of us make full use of it. Everyone could have intelligent tastebuds if these were simply given adequate stimuli and allowed to have their say every now and then, rather than kept in a state of perpetual subjugation, their contacts strictly censored. You can't expect tastebuds conditioned to only mild processed cheese to be overjoyed by Roquefort or Gippsland blue.

The faculty of taste discrimination might be, in the case of a wine judge, the result of long training and experience, but children too have extraordinary abilities. After insisting on cheddar for the first few months we lived in France, my daughter suddenly decided she liked camembert – which was a great relief, since Bega Vintage cheddar was not exactly abundant in the local market. After a while I resented her demanding, and getting, more than her share of my excellent Normandy camembert, individually made in the traditional way from fresh, unpasteurised Normandy milk. Craftily, I devised a solution: I would buy her a camembert all of her own, still a Normandy camembert and perfectly acceptable, but less expensive, a slightly inferior supermarket style of camembert. She would be impressed with having a whole cheese to herself, I reasoned, and wouldn't taste the difference. I presented my daughter, then just past her second birthday, with her camembert in its little wooden box: this is your own camembert, all for you. Hardly had I returned to the table to broach my own cheese when she arrived, plate in hand, to tell me: This camembert is *pas bon*, I want some of yours.

It is incongruous that children are given every opportunity to cultivate whatever musical, artistic, theatrical or sporting talents they have, while the education of the palate is ignored, as if its social value were ignominiously low. Yet cooking schools and wine appreciation courses flourish, and food and wine magazines are avidly read. When the bottom falls out of the economy, cookbooks still survive. Diane Seed, author of several best-selling books on Italian cuisine, remarked that in Italy and other Mediterranean countries (and she could have included Asian countries among her examples), children eat pretty much the same food as adults, at the same times. (In Europe, to compensate for the lateness of the evening meal, the children are given a substantial after-school snack, like the traditional bread-and-chocolate '*goûter*' in France.) Allowed to participate in the meal from an early age, they absorb the gastronomic 'code' of their culture; included in the conversation, they come to appreciate subtleties of taste and texture, the harmony of specific partnerings. As they grow up, they imbibe a gastronomic consciousness which, in later years, turns to confidence.

Jacques Puisais, of the Institut Français du Goût (French Institute of Taste), believes profoundly in the importance of the 'sensory awakening'. Once we have made our senses wake up, he says, we will be immune to the insidious messages of advertising. For years, he and

•

•

his team have been offering 'tasting' classes in primary schools, teaching young children the hows and whats and whys of flavour. (The ideal age is around ten, before puberty starts to interfere.) Since 1990 these tasting classes have been conducted under the auspices of the Conseil National des Arts Culinaires (National Council of Culinary Arts),with support from the Ministry of Education, and tens of thousands of French children have had their senses, intelligence and critical faculties 'awakened'. Over a series of ten 90-minute classes, the children train their senses, and learn to decipher the messages conveyed by colours, odours and textures. Chapped and slightly brown edges on a camembert, together with a faint smell of ammonia, tell them unmistakably that the cheese is way past its prime. Food always offers a choice, Jacques Puisais contends, and taking advantage of the opportunity is to our benefit. If he can persuade even five per cent of the population to 'listen to their bodies', Puisais believes he can begin to effect change – and the process should start within the family. He cites with relish the remark of one young convert to his father: 'Turn the television off, I can't hear what I'm eating.'

Why does he bother? Why does it matter that people know how to taste? Why listen to the message from the senses? Because the senses enrich our lives, add another dimension to the intellect, offer us more to enjoy. We don't need to adopt the extreme philosophy of the Italian futurist Marinetti, whose ideal was simultaneous super-stimulation of the senses. According to one of his recipes, people would be eating black olives, white fennel hearts and orange cumquats with their right hand and caressing with the left hand a 'tactile rectangle' made up of alternating strips of sandpaper, pink silk and black velvet, all the while listening to the music of Bach combined with the sound of an aeroplane motor and as they are surreptitiously sprayed with violet perfume on the nape of the neck. For Marinetti sensory stimulation was vital for energising and lightening the body.

Marinetti's recipe might not be to everyone's taste. To live in a monotonous world of standardised flavours would be like living in a prison, unhealthy for both mind and body. Our senses and our brain are inestimable gifts, and not to respect, encourage and profit from them seems to me almost criminal. We should listen to our senses, understand them, and learn to trust them.

All this is to underline the importance of flavour – 'looking for flavour' could be a metaphor for life. Somewhere beyond Milk Wood, the long-drowned companions of Captain Cat keep asking, in their plaintive seaweedy voices, 'What's the smell of parsley?'

TASTE AND CULTURE

Every country possesses, it seems, the sort of cuisine it deserves,
which is to say the sort of cuisine it is appreciative enough
to want. — Waverley Root

'WHY DO WE EAT?' ask Hsiang Ju Lin and Tsuifeng Lin, authors of *Chinese Gastronomy* (1969). 'In order to pursue the flavour of things,' comes their ready response. But why do we eat what we eat in the way that we do? You might as well ask, 'What is good?'

What we eat is at least circumscribed by the available food supply – or what we deem to be 'food', which introduces additional complications. Most of us don't include insects in our food basket, but in Japan fried grasshoppers and boiled wasp larvae feature on restaurant menus. *Why* we eat these foods in the way we eat them – how we prepare and cook particular foods – invites considerations of culture, in all its subtle intricacies, and its influence on taste. If two cooks in two identical kitchens are given two identical baskets of food, you can bet your bottom dollar they will produce two entirely different meals. Likewise, the same ingredient inspires different dishes in different cultures: compare Peruvian ways with potatoes with Spanish treatments, spicy Indian specialities and the boiled and mashed favourites of the Irish. Such examples suggest that culture is of overriding influence. And looking into our own backyard, what did the Brits do with kangaroo tail but turn it into soup, as they had done for years with oxtail.

With culture come tastes – a taste for a butter-based cuisine in the north of France and an oil-based one in the south. Jean-Pierre, my vigneron friend from the Languedoc region of southern France, told me that eggs fried in butter – which he'd been given when doing his military service in northern Normandy – made him physically sick. At home, his eggs had always been fried in oil, and this was the way he liked them. His preference for oil over butter was not just an expression of individual taste but a reflection of cultural taste that has persisted over many hundreds of years.

Centuries ago, the south of France had oil, but little if any butter, while the north of France produced plenty of butter but little if any oil. Nevertheless, as good Catholics, both southerners and northerners were bound to abstain from animal foods during Lent and on other 'fast days' decreed by the Church. This would hardly have been a penance to the southerners, who were accustomed to cooking with olive oil, but it certainly was for the northerners, who were used to butter. Possibly the southerners kept the best olive oil for themselves and what was available to the northerners was of poor quality or even rancid. When obliged to use this poor-quality oil instead of their own butter in cooking fish, legumes and fresh vegetables, the northerners did so with mumblings of resentment. This probably explains why they were more likely to poach their fish than fry them in the Mediterranean manner. As soon as they found a weakness in the Church's authority, the northern French exploited it. In Rouen today you can still see the remnants of a *'tour de beurre'*, a tower erected with the money the Church received in exchange for dispensation from the 'no butter in Lent' directive.

Distinctive cultural tastes such as these have led researchers Paul and Elizabeth Rozin to describe cuisines according to particular flavour combinations or 'flavour principles' – so that tomato and chilli mean Mexico, and soy sauce, ginger and rice wine characterise China. But tastes in food and drink change over time. Individual tastes evolve through a lifetime, irrespective of what might be happening to public taste; a child has a sweeter tooth than an adult. Public taste can also change; and by public taste I mean a universal taste, the shared tastes or preferences of groups of individuals, whether whole nations or particular regions.

In Australia in the first half of the twentieth century public taste shifted from mutton to lamb. A definite preference for lamb became evident around the 1930s and, if you accept the evidence of cook books, by the 1950s mutton was virtually extinct (though the statistics of the Australian Meat and Livestock Corporation tells us we still get through around 7 kg each per year). Clearly, availability was an important determinant. It is difficult to express a taste for a food that is as scarce as hens' teeth, and in nineteenth-century Australia lamb was a rarity, as mutton is today and as pork is in Morocco. Still, if there had been more demand for lamb, it should have been easy to supply it since the shift in taste seems to have occurred well after the development of a dedicated fat lamb industry – which was established to serve the interests of *British* consumers – made lamb much more accessible.

The disaffection for spices in seventeenth-century France offers another illustration of a genuine shift in taste which also influenced the direction of culinary evolution. No one would dispute the medieval taste for spices; even those who couldn't afford daily extravagances with cinnamon, cardamom and cloves would, for special feasts, pur-chase a minute quantity of a pre-ground (and probably adulterated) spice blend. Yet a few hundred years later, when spices were less costly, palates had recoiled from these bold combinations and turned to the more delicate flavours of herbs, mushrooms, shallots, truffles and other indigenous products. According to historian Jean-Louis Flandrin, part of the explanation lies in the fact that a fall in prices had robbed spices of their role as social markers. Another possibility is that French cuisine attempted to assert its superiority by eschewing oriental influences and vaunting home-grown ingredients.

These examples suggest that shifts in food preferences coincide with other changes in society's values, structures and beliefs, and might even be independent of the supply, or potential availability, of the particular foods. Consider Australians' embracing of Asian foods today, when a century ago anything associated with the Chinese was regarded with deep suspicion. Perhaps the preference for butter in northern France was as much an expression of disenchantment with the Church, distrust of southerners and disgust at rancid oil, as it was a liking for the local product.

Yet it has long been accepted as axiomatic that food preferences flow directly from the food supply. National food policies are predicated on the rationale that offering people more 'healthy' foods and making 'healthy' foods more accessible will necessarily change the national diet in a more 'healthy' direction. If the availability of food is the prime determinant, why do people starve in the midst of plenty, as almost happened in the early days of the first white settlement in Australia?

Food preferences and tastes do not always lend themselves to such straightforward explications. We are people, after all, not robots, and our behaviour is sometimes capricious. We eat hot chillies, and some of us actually enjoy them, yet capsaicin, the essential component, burns and causes pain. People show a distinct liking for chilli-energised foods in tropical parts of Asia where, for personal comfort as much as anything else, it is desirable to reduce body temperature. A theory of biological rationalism has been invoked to account for this particular preference. Its logic is elementary: sweating can cool the body, and chillies cause sweating, therefore people eat chillies and develop a taste for them.

Now, one of the fundamental principles of physics involves the tendency for disorder to rearrange itself as order, and it would be very reassuring to think that Nature, too, has a compensatory bent, such that in hot climates it has favoured ingredients which promote sweating. The difficulty is that chillies don't seem to have arrived in the Asian sub-continent until the sixteenth century or later, and it's not certain that the new chilli-users were aware of any physiological benefits from eating food laced with chillies, nor that they included chillies so as to take advantage of these benefits. (Indeed, it is not even certain that in the chilli's natural habitat, the hot tropics and cooler highlands of the central Americas, people ate chillies and incorporated them into their cuisines in order to enhance their personal comfort.)

A more plausible explanation for the heat of much South East Asian food is that chillies were introduced as, or gradually became, a substitute for pepper, a spice native to many regions that adopted chillies so enthusiastically. Given that the spice trade is one of the world's oldest, it would be surprising to learn that peppercorns were freely available to anyone who ventured into the jungle. Pepper was such an important article of trade for some Asian centres in the medieval centuries that its supply and commerce would surely have been controlled by a merchant elite, and pepper would have been a luxury ingredient that the poorer classes probably had little opportunity to savour. Chillies, on the other hand, belonged to the 'natural' economy of self-sufficiency and were effectively free. Anyone with a scrap of land could grow a few plants, enough to keep the household in chillies for a whole year. They were easy enough to dry and store, and they perked up the relatively monotonous and bland diet which seems always to be the lot of the poor. Who would not have embraced them – especially if using chillies was a way for the workers to show some independence from their bosses, the landowning ruling classes.

This replacement theory might account for the taste for chillies in many parts of Asia, but why do people in Mexico and other countries of the New World like chillies in their cuisines? To return to the availability hypothesis, is the answer simply that chillies are native to that region, as are olive trees in Mediterranean France, syrup-producing maples in Quebec? And does a coincidence of this kind imply a natural affinity, a kind of symbiosis, between the land and the people?

Traditional tastes are are often held to be determined by the natural food environment, by what is grown, produced and available locally. Such geographical determinism is persuasive – and it is undeniable that many examples can be produced to show that people eat, or have eaten, the way they do or did because the range of ingredients produced dictate it. It could be argued that the preference for an oil-based cuisine in southern France was, and even is, the inevitable result of material circumstances. On the other hand, it could also be argued that the foods grown, hunted, harvested and eaten are a reflection of the preferences and tastes of the people.

Applying geographical determinism today, Michael Symons has proposed that what and how we eat in Australia ought perhaps relate to a hypothetical food environment: the ingredients produced in similar climates in other parts of the world. In *The Shared Table* (1993) he suggests that Sydneysiders, living in the same climatic zone as the southern Chinese, might consider eating in a similar way to them. The idea deserves serious consideration, at least from a theoretical viewpoint, since Sydney can assure the ingredients that form the culinary substrate of southern China – pork and vegetables, seafood and ginger. But what was done with them there was influenced by the availability of fuel, by religious beliefs and by contact with the foods and foodways of other regions and countries. The way the people eat in southern China results from the application, by the inhabitants, of these ideas and influences to the material resources. Certainly we have the same foods in Sydney; we can easily borrow the foodways; we can reproduce the southern Chinese cuisine. Yet our relationship to this cuisine is at several removes. We can appreciate it, enjoy it, encourage it – but as mere passive recipients. It is the product of a culture not our own.

It is irrational 'culture' – a product of irrational individuals – that somehow enshrines and perpetuates eating habits. Even when material characteristics frame food preferences, culture makes such eating habits respected, and in this way turns them into traditions. In France, the force of tradition is such that, even though you can buy butter in Mediterranean Béziers as readily as olive oil in Yvetôt in Normandy, the butter–oil division persists. Such tastes become part of a region's identity, the mainstay of its gastronomic character. The substrate, the ingredients produced and available in the region, will almost certainly evolve; some foods will fade away and others take their place. Culture and tradition will shape the way these foods are used, and as these evolve so, too, will tastes and cuisines.

So why do we eat what we eat in the way that we do? Because that's the way we were born, the way we are – and because we like those flavours.

TASTES OF AUSTRALIA PAST

Mrs Wild's 'Evening in Paris' menu featured bouillabaisse accompanied by chicken rice-a-riso.

SO FIRMLY ENTRENCHED are food preferences that we that we expect shifts in taste to be slow and gradual, almost imperceptible in anyone's lifetime. Yet to today's café society the menus of a generation or so ago might appear as foreign as the foods of Elizabethan England. Grilled grapefruit and fried bananas, sherried mushrooms and sherry chiffon pie have gone the way of Frank's chicken pie (with hard-boiled eggs and blanched almonds) and Mother McKay's Heavenly Hash (a daring combination of marshmallows, canned crushed pineapple, sliced bananas, dates and glacé cherries, delicately folded through whipped cream). These were the dishes of the 1960s, as evidenced by the recipes in the *Australian Hostess Cookbook*.

In 1968 the weekly magazine *Woman's Day* conducted a 'Hostess of the Year' contest and, from the thousands of entries received, selected forty of the best to be published as the *Australian Hostess Cookbook*, a superb social document that sets the scene of Australian entertaining in the Swinging Sixties. Forty menus, forty dinner plans, forty lists of Things To Do, forty descriptions of My Dinner Party – from every state, from capital cities and remote country properties, all proud testimonies of hostessing savoir-faire and affirmations of the proper division of domestic roles: she in the kitchen, he at the bar. These were the days when Dressing for Dinner meant exactly that, when there was such a thing as the Dinner Dress. Preferred dress for dinner parties was, it seems, 'semi-formal' – and people instinctively knew this meant lounge suits for men and, for women, 'either short dinner dresses, hostess skirts and tops, or long dresses'.

There was a precise protocol to the Dinner Party, an emphasis on form and formality and a tacit acknowledgement of the Rules of Entertaining of which the prime one, unchallengeable in its absoluteness, was Be Prepared! Hostesses must be proficient in the arts of planning, preparation and presentation, decreed Mrs Robson. All the plates, forks, spoons, glasses, wine coasters and ashtrays likely to be used must be polished and assembled in readiness. The whole dinner party should unfold in the hostess's imagination; the unforeseen was simply not allowed. As Mrs Joye curtly admonished, 'There is nothing worse than a hostess who starts digging around in cupboards while her guests are present.' Preparation started as much as a week in advance

•

•

to leave plenty of time, on the morning of the Dinner Party, to have your hair set, arrange the flowers, spray the rooms with freshener, put out hand towels and leave a needle and cotton on the dressing table in case a guest should catch the hem of her long skirt on a stiletto heel.

The men, as usual, had charge of the drinks. In the alcohol department, they were allowed to be creative and imaginative (elsewhere, it appears, they simply obeyed the rules). Mrs Joye offered her husband's 'very popular and successful' recipe for champagne cocktails: a bottle of champagne, a cup of brandy, half a cup of canned orange juice, a teaspoon of bitters and crushed ice. Mr Joye would serve this 'from a large cut-glass bowl with a silver ladle into hollow-stemmed cut-glass champagne glasses, which he frosts with his latest acquisition – a glass chiller.' Men were accessories, unpaid butlers. 'Train your man early,' advised Mrs Robson, 'he's worth a kitchenful of time-saving devices.' Mr Robson's 'party chores' included setting out and polishing all the glasses, taking responsibility for drinks, and filling the pre-dinner nut bowls with cashews.

These were the days when for Mrs Curr's yabby cocktail Aboriginal boys could be 'dispatched to get about two dozen yabbies from the lagoon or river. They enjoy swimming quietly up and thrusting their hands quickly into the holes in the banks where the yabbies are half-hidden'. They were the brown-and-orange days of Arabia platters and rustic pottery, the days of chicken à la king, onion dip and liverwurst canapés, the days when hostesses had no qualms about offering lounge-suited guests tomato soup and cream of chicken soup straight from Edgell or Rosella, or including in their recipes canned mushrooms, frozen peas, packet soups and commercial hamburger seasoning. Mrs Wild's 'Evening in Paris' menu featured bouillabaisse accompanied by chicken rice-a-riso. Canned fruits and commercial icecreams made respectable desserts.

Some of the dishes of those Swinging Sixties have disappeared without regret – the Iced Camembert and Asparagus Fromage. Others, such as Roast Saddle of Lamb and Strawberries Romanoff are waiting in the wings to be resurrected, like that 1920s hit, Steak Diane. The roundabout of fashion acts as powerfully on our tastes in food as on heel heights and lipstick colours. Regardless of their merit, dishes go out of fashion and become forgotten. Amongst them are crumbed cutlets and carpetbag steak, two dishes which are as much a part of our gastronomic heritage as Milk Arrowroot biscuits and chocolate Freddo Frogs, and whose return to our culinary cornucopia would be welcomed. The stew, on the other hand, might not be missed.

CRUMBED CUTLETS

Once upon a time, crumbed cutlets appeared on all the best dinner tables – and on the lunch counters of every pub west of the Divide. Cookbook author Ted Moloney included them (seasoned, and wrapped in bacon before crumbing) in one of his 'Cooking for Brides' menus. Along with the redoubtable Caramel Sauce, they were a perennial on the menu of all Cahill's Sydney restaurants in the 1950s, and I'm sure they enjoyed a moment of *amour propre* in the rarefied atmosphere of Adams' Silver Grill dining room. They persisted as a weekly special in university colleges and other institutions. Sometimes, no doubt, the crumbs concealed squalors better left concealed (as they often do on today's ubiquitous squid rings), but is that any reason to consign crumbed cutlets to the back of the fridge, along with all the other *restes* of yesterday?

•

•

Not so long ago, for a simple family meal, I prepared crumbed cutlets using proper lamb that I carefully trimmed of all external fat and coated in proper breadcrumbs that I had toasted to the warm gold of Sydney sandstone. Anticipating the pleasure of eating an old favourite, I was unprepared for the shock-horror reaction my menu announcement provoked. Crumbed cutlets, unfortunately, do not make it into today's top 100. If I'd announced sauteed barramundi liver with wattle seed *beurre blanc*, I'd probably have received a beam of approval.

I suspect that in the fervour for Frenchness (in food) that followed in the wake of Elizabeth David's *French Provincial Cooking*, a Frenchness that was well and truly evident in the *Australian Hostess Cookbook*, the crumbed cutlet went the way of stockings, hats and gloves – only to be reincarnated as the *carré d'agneau*, or 'French rack of lamb', which introduced us to lamb as we always knew it should be eaten, a sliver of garlic between each flank, daringly pink. Later again, in the post-French Provincial phase glorified by the revolutionary catch-cry of 'nouvelle cuisine', the *carré* – by then divested of both its crumbs and its proud handles – metamorphosed into the elegant lamb fillet.

Yet in the prospering bourgeois era of the turn of the century, crumbed cutlets (which, then, were not lamb but mutton) were reassuringly correct. They were always accompanied by mashed potatoes – 'Dish round a border of mashed potatoes,' instructs Mrs Forster Rutledge in *The Goulburn Cookery Book* – and sometimes served with gravy. Curiously, they seem to be more of a tradition in the eastern States. South Australian butchers rarely sell crumbed cutlets, nor even the undressed ones. At a time when regional cuisines are desperately sought, New South Wales might be as proud of its crumbed cutlets as Milan of its *costolette milanese*!

It might symbolise the soul-destroying regularity of middle-class suburbia, or remind us of a colonial and Anglo-dominated past we'd rather forget, but these are not reasons to decree extinction for the innocent crumbed lamb cutlet. Properly prepared, the crumbed cutlet merits a second chance. Tastes change, certainly, but the fate of any dish should not depend solely on the whims of fashion and the vagaries of medical wisdom.

CARPETBAG STEAK

If it was a bold man who first ate an oyster, it was an ingenious one who first thought of stuffing oysters in a steak.

As one of Australia's contributions to the world's gastronomic treasure house, carpetbag steak has often been derided and disdained as a dish people would rather not lay claim to – like a convict past, before bicentennial fervour arrived. Together with damper and billy tea, pan jam and slippery bob (which, for the uninitiated, were said to be dishes of kangaroo tail and kangaroo brains, respectively), it is part of the national mythology, the culinary counterpart to the bunyip.

Steak-and-oysters has a long history, and the English were well accustomed to this early manifestation of the surf'n'turf combination. Oysters went into beefsteak pies, oyster sauce accompanied grilled steaks. It seems to have been a predilection peculiar to the English, for while the French *Larousse Gastronomique* gives a recipe for oyster sauce to serve with steak it coyly calls it '*à l'anglaise*', English-style. Yet the idea of internalising the oysters seems to have been an antipodean inspiration, as was the name; the 1962 edition of Mrs Beeton's cookbook gave carpetbag steak as an Australian recipe. In America a carpet bag was strictly that – a travelling bag made of carpeting – though Americans might have eaten carpetbag steak under another name, since in 1907 a recipe for tenderloins stuffed with oysters was included in the *Women's Favourite Cookbook*, by Mrs Gregory and Friends. In Australia a recipe entitled simply 'Carpet Bag' appeared in the earliest *Presbyterian Cookery Book*, published in Sydney at the end of the nineteenth century: two dozen plump oysters in a thick piece of steak, grilled over the coals and sauced with anchovy butter. Several years later Mrs Rutledge (who seems to have had a fondness for embellishment) christened her recipe 'Carpet-bag a la Colchester', as if to give it the semblance of noble and legitimate ancestry, Colchester being an English town famous for its oysters (they were the ones that once travelled as far as imperial Rome).

Perhaps the name Carpet Bag didn't really take off, or was thought to be slightly disreputable, like the American carpetbaggers who were said to own nothing but what was in their carpet bags. Having been kept alive through a number of revisions of the book, the recipe was axed from the *Presbyterian Cookery Book* around 1927, but the dish, even stripped of its epithet, lived on anonymously. Local ladies, apparently ignorant of the appellation, contributed recipes for fillet steak stuffed with oysters to *The Kookaburra Cookery Book* in 1911 and to Miss Futter's *Australian Home Cookery* in 1923, which would seem to be adequate proof that the dish existed in the flesh, so to speak. Even the redoubtable Lady Hackett, in 1916, prescribed a recipe in her *Australian Household Guide* (having indelicately lifted it from the *Kookaburra*).

Meanwhile, back in England, the Brits stuck to their beefsteak-

and-oyster stews and pies and puddings. It was not until 1952 that Florence White published, in her record of 'Famous Food and Drink of Yesterday and Today', a recipe for Saddle-bag Steaks that was virtually identical to that for the earliest carpetbag. Of course, it's possible that the Saddle-bag Steak existed previously, or that it evolved independently, but it is curious that most earlier English cookbooks and dining memoirs neglect it. Can we claim carpetbag steak as our first culinary conquest? Enthusiastic visions of exporting the kangaroo steamer, which so impressed early visitors to Tasmania, were never realised; lamingtons and anzac biscuits are largely unknown outside Australia – even the standard sponge has to be copiously footnoted for an American audience; and the meat pie invasion of Asia is of much more recent date.

Consider the reputation of carpetbag steak. Is it such a travesty of taste as to deserve ignominy? In true scientific spirit, I prepared Carpet Bag according to the recipe in the *Presbyterian Cookery Book*, grilled it over a beautiful bed of red gum coals and topped it with disks of anchovy butter (and, just for the record, accompanied it with braised warrigal greens, green beans, new potatoes cooked in butter and an aged Gigondas). Admittedly, the sample size was not so large as to submit to statistical scrutiny, and the system of evaluation was not standardised, but the universal appraisal was 'Delicious!' The steak was pink, the oysters just warm, and their sea-saltiness subtly permeated the whole. The flavour combination seemed as natural as tomato and basil, or prosciutto and melon, or strawberries and cream.

But perhaps to make the carpetbag truly and authentically Australian, I should make one small modification: Take a thick slab of kangaroo fillet . . .

•

•

S T E W

Calling a spade a spade is supposed to be defiantly Australian. It reassures us that we're totally lacking in pretension. Today, however, anyone with the meekest of bourgeois aspirations prefers the euphonious casserole to the unworldly stew. As uncool as Joylene's Frock Salon, stew belongs to the never-to-be-resurrected past, the pre-quiche era of mornays, sausage rolls and toothpicked cheese cubes alternating with gaudy green and red onions. Though stew is a kitchen table kind of meal, perfectly at home in the shearers' mess, and we never imagine it joining this illustrious company of entertainers.

No doubt good cooks knew how to prepare a tasty stew, but the generic version must have been a sorry sight, and even more dismal to eat. As Dr Henry Priestley observed in 1936, 'In the cooking of dishes like a stew they [i.e. housewives] mostly choose chopped up steak, maybe some flour, some water, and a little salt. They put it on the stove, and hope for the best. They seldom take any steps to bring out the flavour.' In 1937 *The Woman's Mirror Cookery Book* offered this recipe for Castlereagh Stew:

> *Two pounds shin of beef, onions, salt and pepper, flour and water. Cut beef into pieces, dip in seasoned flour, put into saucepan and just cover with cold water to which has been added 1 tablespoon vinegar to each quart. Bring to boil, then simmer 3 hours, cutting up 2 onions and adding them two hours after cooking begins. Calories: 1643, Protein: 206, Fat: 62, Carbohydrate: 45, Vitamin quality, Medium B1, B2.*

This was the standard and definitive method of making a stew, officially corroborated by health authorities. According to the New South Wales Department of Public Health in 1963, a 'stew' is made with meat, onions, seasonings and/or herbs, covered with cold water and simmered 2-3 hours, then thickened with flour or cornflour.

These recipes make stew sound as cheerless and uninspiring as we somehow suspected it must always have been – grey, gluggy, mundane and utterly misery-making. Why should such a depressing dish have ever entered our repertoire? Where were the tastebuds at that time? If anywhere, tastebuds seem to have been in purgatory, banished and suppressed from fear of the repercussions should they have been allowed their liberty. In the early decades of this century, 'plain food' was synonymous with moral rectitude, small 'p' puritanism – and the plainer the food, the more virtuous the eater. Titillating the palate was as dangerous as lifting your skirts, and the list of gustatory temptations was nearly as long as the catalogue of sins: salt, spices, sauces and any flavourings that might have cheered the senses were all feared and proscribed by the Plain Food lobby. It was the same in England, and Elizabeth David's first book, *Mediterranean Food* (1950), was begun as 'a furious revolt against that terrible, cheerless, heartless food' served by the English hotel in which she was staying. (She described it as food 'produced with a kind of bleak triumph which amounted almost to a hatred of humanity and humanity's needs.')

No wonder there was an eventual rebellion, a move to demonstrate some gastronomic good sense by introducing the glamorous 'casserole' which appeared on middle-class tables as an honourable alternative to roasts, grills and shepherd's pie. Casseroles suggested smartness; they were modern and respectable and even labour-saving, the cooking pot doubling as serving dish. And while the casserole was a meat-in-gravy kind of dish, it was not simply a gentrified stew, rebaptised with a new name. What defined a stew was that it cooked on top of the stove and, typically, was thickened at the end (or, alternatively, had dumplings added to it). A casserole, on the other hand, cooked in the oven. The trademark of a casserole recipe was the final phrase: 'Serve in the dish in which it has been cooked'. It's hardly a coincidence that this evolutionary phase occurred around the same time that Pyrex oven-to-table ware was featuring more often at kitchen teas and as marriage prizes, around the same time that gas and electric stoves and their automatic ovens were supplanting wood-fired anachronisms in the kitchen. Nor is a coincidence that its modernity appealed to the food industry, whose packet seasonings could provide the means for even the clumsiest cook to produce a tasty casserole of any nationality.

Of course the casserole didn't entirely supplant the stew, and there are some perfectly reputable stews, such as oxtail stew. But stew still carries with it hints of an inglorious past, the days of shame when pleasure was almost a dirty word. Let's redeem the stew, allow it to stay in our culinary lexicon, but on condition that it gets itself a whole new wardrobe and dresses itself with aromatic herbs and vegetables, with spices and wine – in other words, with flavour.

THE FASCINATION OF MARKETS

*Why do we need markets? Because the informal interchanges
provoked by a pile of fresh young artichokes are hardly
possible at a supermarket.*

HOW TO EXPLAIN the fascination of markets? For fascination there undoubtedly is – who can resist the open-handed invitation of a market, whether a casual cluster of tables beneath spreading trees or a cavernous, sweaty hall whose earthy aura proclaims both its character and its function?

Markets have been part of my life for almost as long as I can remember, from the days when I accompanied my grandfather to the old Sydney Paddy's Markets for his Christmas lychees and Chinese jars of ginger in syrup, one day getting lost when I lingered too long with the puppies and chickens. Paddy's on Fridays was a regular outing during school holidays, though there was a sense of something not quite respectable about buying cheese and bacon at a market stall, especially from people you couldn't understand (though the same doubts did not apply to the rock-like candy we bought). In later years I – together with about half of Sydney – would descend on Paddy's Market for the traditional box of Bowen mangoes for Christmas. Later again, travelling overseas, markets were always an excuse to stop and explore. Better than any guidebook, they told me about people and their everyday lives, what they grow and how they eat. Today a visit to the market is still part of my week.

I have a passion for markets, for shopping at markets. I like the feeling of food around me, the comfort of plenty. I like the sense of egality markets presume, and their sensory appeal goes direct to the core of my being. I am moved by scents of mangoes and durian and roasting coffee, of sugary fritters in the morning air, of spicy sacrificial smoke from noonday *souvlaki*. I love the chaos of colours and shapes and noise – the chatter of hens in wicker cages alongside somnolent rabbits, the clamour of spruikers, the lurching rumble of laden trolleys. And I participate, joining in spontaneous exchanges on the merits of maragogype versus mocha or the effects of last night's rain on the cherry crop, because markets promote communication and allow everyone to have a say. For as much as foods, markets are people, offering sustenance not only to individuals but to society.

The market is a meeting place, a natural community centre where goodwill pervades. It's not only the colours, sounds and smells of a market that cheer, but the gratifying sight of so many people enjoying themselves. Friday evening at Adelaide's Central Market sees families meet and shop, children participating in decisions and counting apples into bags. At this relaxed end of the week working couples gather ingredients for the evening's dinner and plan the weekend meals. Saturday morning shoppers meet friends and pause for a leisurely coffee. The same casual friendliness prevails at Darwin's Mindil Beach sunset market. It seems that half the city's population congregates to sit back on the beach, applaud the spectacle of the sunset and sample street food from over twenty nationalities, from Thai-style stuffed chicken wings to Brazilian sardines with polenta, to Laotian fish cakes made with the local barramundi.

The appeal of a market sometimes lies in our desire for a closer communion with Nature. At markets we persuade ourselves that the privilege of buying from producers themselves links us with the land and gives our purchases a seal of authenticity. We assume that by avoiding rapacious middlemen and perfidious marketing experts, we've made a fair deal, our choices uninfluenced by advertising promises or flattering lights or pretty packaging. We tell ourselves that markets subscribe to the simplest economic system, where trans-actions are up-front and direct. Our anti-authoritarian tendencies are gratified by the individuality of markets, which follow their own rules and logic in a kind of benevolent anarchy, most evident in open-air weekend markets. Long before supermarkets and shops were allowed to trade on Sunday, markets flourished, usually outside the cities and often outside the law.

At markets we acknowledge a deep-seated faith in the honesty of fellow citizens and the justice of what-you-see-is-what-you-get. We don't need to read labels or compare ingredient lists, because our senses make the selections. Thus liberated, we can enjoy a rare experience of the simple life, where the only decisions that matter are between camembert and brie, between snapper cutlets and tommy ruff, between Desiree potatoes at two dollars a kilo and a bag of anonymous unwashed for fifty cents. And immediately we have chosen we know, instinctively, that the choice was right.

Why are there so few markets in Australian towns and cities? When Ildefons Cerdà drew up his plans for the expansion of Barcelona in 1860, he included a general market for every unit, a ten-block by ten-block square. Now that shopping hours in Australia are deregulated, why do we not have small community markets as in Paris, for example, where weekly street markets co-exist with the Monday-to-Saturday supermarkets around the corner? Why not late afternoon and evening markets for the parents who have just collected children from school and the workers returning home from the city? Why not markets at universities, factories, and other locations where a sizeable, ready-made collection of customers exists? Why not Sunday producers' markets in the cities, where producers and consumers can actually make contact? When supermarket 'fresh' might just as well mean 'week-old', surely there's room for alternatives.

Why do we need markets? Because markets offer social as well as physical sustenance and stimulation. Because they offer choice, or the illusion of choice. Because the informal interchanges provoked by a pile of fresh young artichokes are hardly possible at a supermarket – where you'd be lucky to find artichokes, and if you did, no one at the checkout would know what they were, or what to do with them. In the

•

•

depths of winter, when depression strikes like the flu, a visit to the market does wonders for the soul.

Once upon a time, so I read, about a century ago, a nobleman in imperial Russia conducted an experiment to study the development of language. Taking advantage of a convenient group of orphans, the eccentric count gave instructions that they were to be properly fed and clothed, and given toys and opportunities for games and play, but were not to be spoken to. They were to be raised without the use of language. Periodically he would visit the nursery to observe, but his experiment was inconclusive since, within a matter of a few years, all the children were dead. If there is a moral here it must surely emphasise the importance of communication.

The socialising benefit of markets was emphasised by the experience of my Parisian landlord a couple of years ago. Georges is a high-powered scientist, working in a large, modern research institute in the suburban belt just south of Paris. Pressure of work and international conferences, together with the alienating atmosphere of a structure dedicated to efficiency, meant that he saw little of his colleagues – and then only in the sterile space of a laboratory. Georges' relaxation was weekend cooking. At that time, he was working his way through Paul Bocuse's *Cuisine du Marché*. While his wife took care of the supermarket goods – jam, sugar, detergent – Georges followed his Saturday morning ritual: a visit to the regular market in nearby Sceaux, with its fish and potatoes direct from Brittany, creamy farm cheeses, fresh vegetables and the superb honey and gingerbread from Burgundy. But just as important as this 'real' food was the social contact of the market. Every Saturday he would bump into one or other of his colleagues, similarly motivated. Shopping finished, they would meet at the café and, over a few beers, exchange ideas and visions in a way they never could at work.

Markets represent, at least in the imagination, a kind of ideal world in microcosm, a focus of humanity. They offer clues to the nature of cultures and societies and illustrate their values. Perhaps nowhere is the contrast between two cultures more visible than at the main Singapore market, where an invisible wall exists between the Malay Muslims on one side, and Chinese stallholders along the other. Each side has its distinctive smells and its particular logic. In the Malay zone, you encounter the warm, spicy, fatty aromas of curries, cooked meats and stale bodies. At butchers' stalls, meat is hacked into gobbets without any reference to the animal's anatomy. The men sitting at tables are as plump and greasy as their mid-morning curry puffs, and seem totally unfazed by the possibility of paying customers. Walk into the Chinese area, and you are greeted by the gentle fragrance of ginger; here is an air of cleanliness, order and propriety. At the poultry stalls, bits and pieces are arrayed according to a code you can comprehend: wings, gizzards, feet, necks. Behind the stands, men and women seem only too eager to help and guide you to a seat before bringing a drink. To extrapolate from such impressions would be unwise and undiplomatic. Yet the differences exist, and it would be foolish to deny any significance.

In the old days, the market was the agora, the forum, the heart of the city. It was the place of exchange – of news and views, plots and intrigues, goods and services. After the cold and comfortless Dark Ages, markets were the spark that reignited the fires of cuisine. Here, in the town's nucleus, local produce was arrayed alongside exotic rarities from foreign lands, their choice and variety stimulating the cook's imagination, while footloose adventurers told tales of feasts and fashions in faraway lands.

For the novelist Emile Zola, the market was the stomach of the city: *le ventre*. The alimentary metaphor conveys the image of foods gradually percolating to all sections of the populace, and Jean-Paul Aron's account of eating in nineteenth-century Paris, *The Art of Eating in France: Manners and menus in the nineteenth century* (1975), shows how this actually occurred. Leftovers and surpluses from grand dinners of the previous evening were recycled through the 17-sous restaurants frequented by poor students and shop assistants, and their leftovers, in turn, made their way through the lower reaches of society by means of markets, street hawkers and scavengers. Today, in Paris and many other cities, the main wholesale market is outside the city – perhaps not so much a stomach as an external life support system for provisioning the city. Such a system needs arteries of distribution, channels of food flow, which in turn means regulation and control.

Most of us are ignorant of the city's stomach, being far more preoccupied with our own – and besides, the city's stomach keeps such uncivilised hours. Our familiarity is with the smaller retail market or the Sunday market on the edge of the city, where suburban fingers extend into the domain of agriculture. Our household provisioning starts there – or, speaking for myself, that's where I prefer to buy the foods I eat and offer to others. There are times when we choose the other extreme, the sterility of a food hall or the standardised selection of a supermarket. There's nothing wrong with food halls and supermarkets – 'a North American supermarket is marketplace, temple, palace all rolled into one,' says Margaret Visser – but, while they do a great job of selling canned grouse from Scotland and 57 varieties of

•

•

breakfast cereal, they don't give you the thrill of a real, live market with real, live food.

How do I justify my predilection for markets in these days of economic rationalism, when attempts are made to describe every conceivable part of life (and, grimly, death) in balance sheet numbers? Were I to be thoroughly objective and carry out a properly controlled comparison, perhaps I'd discover that the difference between market and supermarket potatoes is illusory, that the portion of cheese freshly cut to my specifications is little different to the vacuum-packed one standing between the yogurts and margarines. Continuing down the path of objectivity, I might report that supermarket shopping has the advantage of being more economical of time – the time needed to assemble the provisions, the transit time between household and provisioning source. Indeed, given that people usually travel individually to markets, the net effect might be to add to already undesirable levels of environmental pollution.

But food choice doesn't lend itself to such analysis. There are times when it is irreproachably rational (I'll take these small yellow peaches at $2.99 a kilo rather than the big ones at $3.99), and others when it is supremely irrational (I *must* have a mango, even if it does come from Indonesia and cost $5, because mangoes are so seductive and remind me of . . .). And what of time? It's only worth economising if what is saved is used more pleasurably or more profitably; you can't hide it under the bed for a rainy day. What price do you put on pleasure? My justification rests on my set of values, which have little regard for economics but set much store on quality – and in food, quality is synonymous with flavour. Unfortunately, flavour is invisible, though it has much to do with freshness and ripeness, two qualities markets can assure. Often it has a visible indicator in the form of price. Though this relationship is neither sufficient nor necessary, it serves as a general rule of thumb and at least makes you pay attention: Why are these peaches a dollar more? Is it only because they're larger? Are they any fresher, more perfumed, more flavoursome?

If I learnt one lesson (but I learnt many) from my years in France, it was this: as a general rule, price and quality are directly proportional – except when the price is fixed by government decree, as it is for bread, in which case you pay the same for superb and just-average baguettes and responsibility for choice is yours. Incidentally, I also discovered that a whole range of qualities was possible, in foods as diverse as pâté and potatoes. And I realised that, with a little practice, it was not too difficult to discern (and appreciate) the difference between moderately good and superior, between mediocre and downright poor.

The most memorable lesson came by way of chicken. I had bought, cooked and eaten chicken in Australia, and at that time chicken – whether fresh or frozen, whole or in pieces – was always the same mass-produced bird that cost hardly more than a couple of dollars. In the 1970s people accepted that it was no longer the celebratory roast that accompanied Christmas and other festive occasions, and approved the democratisation which transferred chicken to the province of everyday. Cut: to the Languedoc, where our new friend Jean-Pierre, from whom we bought our wine, also sold dressed chickens every Friday, *jour de marché* in his village of Caux. Jean-Pierre was proud of his indecently ugly birds with the bare necks and backsides characteristic of the '*cou nu*' breed, and sold them at about 16 francs a kilo (then, about twenty years ago, near enough to $3).

•

•

This was our first home-cooked French *poulet,* and we were impressed: firm-textured meat of distinct, robust flavour, and plenty of it. I found it tremendously reassuring to discover that the French had not forgotten their taste buds.

Now, though we weren't quite poverty-stricken, we did have to watch our centimes very carefully, and so the next time I bought chicken I chose one from the Saturday Pézenas market at about the half the price, which was still slightly more expensive than one from the supermarket. After Jean-Pierre's lovingly nurtured chicken, the market bird – which, as usual, came with attached head and feet and much of its insides – was disappointing, its flavour muddied and indistinct. Yet this market chicken with its slightly dirty toenails (the great chef Michel Guérard once confided to his television audience that the best way to tell whether a bird had been naturally raised and had scratched for a living was to check its toenails for farmyard dirt) was sublime compared to the cheapest chicken I have ever bought – a pack of assorted pieces, on special at a Minneapolis supermarket. I hate to think of the processes to which these chicken pieces had been subjected to make them so flavourless and full of water – let alone what kind of life the poor birds had endured.

Markets don't always, don't necessarily, provide the absolute best quality, but they typically offer the best *range* of qualities and usually, for equivalent quality, a cheaper product. With quality, remember, we are talking flavour which, for fruits and vegetables in particular, depends on freshness and ripeness. Freshness means more than simply being raw, unprocessed and still in birthday suits; it assumes a minimum delay between farm and market. Whether figs or fish – and particularly so for fish – freshness means flavour. Ripeness implies that the produce has been allowed to stay on the plant long enough to get as close as possible to the point of optimum flavour. Because markets can respond immediately to production flushes, and because they usually operate from day to day (they don't plan 'specials' a week or so in advance), their fresh produce is more likely to be fresher and riper than that of the supermarket.

I remember with horror – and, now, shame at having succumbed to the temptation – the Californian strawberries advertised in Minneapolis at the local Red Owl supermarket at such a low, low price that I began to wonder what truck they had fallen off. After the chicken experiment, I didn't usually patronise that establishment, but in the snow-bound depths of a mid-western winter, when the monotony of oranges/apples/bananas had become too depressing, the idea of ripe, red strawberries from sunny California beckoned seductively. And so, early on the first day of the week, there I was at the supermarket, arriving at the same time as a huge refrigerated container rolled in with goods for the store's coolroom. Inside the store, swanking on a stand all to themselves, punnets of blushing red strawberries were piled high. I perused and examined and compared this punnet with that before choosing the one which promised so much pleasure – not only for myself, but for my family, whose delight at this unexpected treat would materialise as a golden halo above my head and confirm me in my role of blessed nurturer. I should have foreseen that unseasonal strawberries transported from one corner of America to another would have to be bred of sterner stuff than the ones I used to buy from barrows in Sydney's Martin Place in October. Fresh? Ripe? Those strawberries were a travesty of freshness and ripeness, and a sad comment on what passes for Progress.

●

●

There are other advantages to markets. Since the goods are usually untouched by plastic or packaging of any form, you don't have to rely on labels; you can see and touch and hear and smell before you buy. The Farmers' Market in the heart of San Francisco began as a revolt against the dominance of supermarkets and their insistence that all oranges and tomatoes, in fact all fruits and vegetables, be cartoned, wrapped and sealed before they would consider buying them. A group of farmers, who saw these demands as another step along the road of subjugation and who believed pre-packaging both unnecessary and undesirable, resisted – only to find themselves shunned by the chains of stores on whom they had previously depended. The only alternatives were to succumb or to go it alone, which they did, maintaining their integrity and independence, and demonstrating their faith in flavour.

Producers' markets like this one are important to 'alternative' agriculture, whether organic or devoted to heritage or specialised varieties not necessarily chosen for their transport endurance. There's no reason why they can't take place in large cities – like San Francisco. Or Paris, where for the past seven years the Marché Biologique has operated every Sunday in the middle of the Boulevard Raspail, beginning near the square opposite the Bon Marché department store and extending towards Montparnasse. By French standards it is small, but most of the stallholders are also the producers, accredited 'natural and organic' by some association or other. Their offerings are strictly seasonal: in winter, different varieties of potatoes, an array of little-known apples, including the *Reinette du Mans*, and wonderfully sweet and juicy, dug-that-day carrots. At this market 'organic' is not limited to fruits and vegetables. There are all kinds of farm-fresh dairy products, from rich cream, yogurt and *fromage frais* to goat cheeses of all shapes and ages. And breads – rustic country loaves, rye and walnut bread, tarts and brioches rather more substantial than the standard-ised patisserie ones. Then honey, fruity jams and home-style preserves, even poultry and meat and *charcuterie biologique*, including organic black pudding. This is a fully-fledged market, right down to its sun-dried salt and homespun wool, serving the needs of Parisians and of the producers.

Markets encourage freedom of choice – these particular peaches, this much cheese, that well-crisped loaf of bread, and and a hunk of this particular pumpkin with the rich orange flesh. They allow more dimensions of choice than is possible in a supermarket, despite its reputed stock of over 15,000 different items. Their unpredictability – strawberries on sale one week and not the next – is part of their charm. They attract a wider, or at least a different, range of growers and producers, including those whose output is insufficient, irregular, or simply too expensive to induce supermarkets to stock it. As buyers and consumers, we have an obligation to make the most of this freedom, to think about the foods we are choosing and why, to reflect on our own tastes and preferences and recognise how best to satisfy them.

But we cannot always be sure of our selection skills, even when we are allowed to feel and sniff, which is why we also rely on the people behind the counters. As specialists, dealing only in cheese, or coffee, or fruits and vegetables, and with a vested interest in their business, they are deemed worthy of our trust – and when it's a question of the foods we allow into our bodies, trust is all-important. We often react to un-familiar foods with caution, an expression of instinctive neophobia:

might it not be dangerous? If we can know the source, or receive assurance from the expert, we have more confidence to try.

Sociability, flavour, trust: there I rest my case for shopping at markets. But what of other people's markets, the markets you explore when you have no intention of provisioning a household, or even a hotel room? Whenever I travel, I visit markets. Indeed, markets come before museums. My wardrobe – if not my pantry – is littered with market purchases: a leather coat from Cambridge, unworn for the last twenty years but too full of memories to discard; a silver chain from Ayutthaya; a hand-knitted wool jacket from Florence, just behind the cathedral. From Lisbon and Leningrad, Boston and Barcelona, Marrakech and Milan, I have my souvenirs to keep company with the elegant oyster-opening knife from the street market in rue Daguerre, Paris. And I have ineffaceable memories – of a warm *tarte aux blettes* from the market at Nice, of an entire carcase strung up before the horse butcher's stall in the market at Taranto. From Asian markets I have images of stalls festooned with plastic bowls, colanders, buckets and brooms in bright primary colours of red, green, blue and yellow; of shoppers carrying home water-filled plastic bags of live carp, still swimming; of mysterious and odd-shaped excrescences on the herbalist's stall in Kuala Lumpur; of dozens of dried fish and prawns in Penang, including dried squid which I later ate on the Penang waterfront, after it had been put through a sort of mangle and barbecued.

How to explain my fascination for markets? It all comes down to a fascination with food, its uses and its meanings. For food can never be simply sustenance for the physical body; it also represents the myths and mores, the priorities and practices of a society.

MARKETS IN SICILY:

A MEDIEVAL PRESENCE

*A tumble of wrinkled black olives is confined behind
a fence of stout rosemary sprigs. The stalls of the
pescivendoli are decorated with the sawn-off heads
of swordfish, and fronds of fresh green fennel
separate the different species of fish.*

LIKE LOVE, TRAVEL can be better the second time around. Though
my letters and notebooks are littered with the names of places I passed
through, with regrets at not stopping, and those where I stayed all too

briefly, Sicily was always one of the destinations to which I intended to return.

My memories of Sicily were of the enormous octopus in the market, cooked and sitting upright on a vast flat platter – itself decorated with an octopus in Arabic blue and yellow – and looking for all the world as though it had risen from the clay. I remembered, too, the pascal sugar lambs in the *pasticcerie*, all white and innocent save for the gaudy garlands of pink and yellow flowers around their necks; and, in an ordinary, modest little cafe, a marvellously refreshing iced coffee, a simple espresso-on-the-rocks, the taste of which lingers still.

But of course, the second time is different, the coincidences never quite coincide. True, I did find the octopus man at the Palermo market, but it was not at the main market; rather, he stood in a small square, near a fountain, in the old part of town – the site of the medieval market. And his plate was an ordinary white dinner plate on which the boiled octopus looked pitifully small. The sugar lambs were now made of sugar-almond paste (though I did find one made of sugar, in a dusty shop not far from the octopus man) and, instead of flowers round their necks, they carried little flags of red or blue. After this, I hardly dared tempt fate with an iced coffee, but stayed with the *caffe lungo* – which in Sicily is as strong and black as the shortest espresso anywhere else, and usually drunk very, very sweet.

For all that, I did rediscover much of what had become vague and blurred and almost forgotten, and experienced – or re-experienced – the same enchantments that had lured me to Sicily the first time: certain primitive, almost naive qualities in Sicilian culture and life in general; a Mediterranean vitality and fatality; and the heritage of its past, subtle and persuasive, which allows the ancient and medieval to co-exist with the contemporary as if to make a mockery of Time.

Sicilian markets are loud and gutsy. In Palermo, the market sprawls through a maze of narrow alleys and odd-shaped 'squares' in the manner of a Moroccan *souk*. Its atmosphere is friendly and reassuring. Nowhere in Palermo did I feel more relaxed, less self-consciously tourist than in its market, and no one came up to me to warn me to hang on to my valuables. The market stands are crude, colourful and enticing. A tumble of wrinkled black olives is confined behind a fence of stout rosemary sprigs.The stalls of the *pescivendoli* are decorated with the sawn-off heads of swordfish, and fronds of fresh green fennel separate the different species of fish. There are familiar ones, such as bream and mullet and John Dory, and a whole array of sea creatures whose size would, in Australian terms, deem them inedible if not illegal. Who said the fad for 'miniatures' in food was a new one? Tiny, tiny octopus (*moscardelle*), their sacs no bigger than the tip of one's little finger, lie curled up against one another; next to them are boxes of baby sardines (*sardelle*), a steely, slippery grey in colour and barely two inches long, and the even smaller *neonate*, milky-translucent slivers with big black eyes. All are gleaming fresh and still smell of the sea. In the days just before Easter, fish is very much on the menu, and *baccalà*, or salt cod, is also for sale – not the desiccated grey strips with which we are familiar and which hang above the counter of Greek or Italian delicatessens, but soft white flesh, pre-soaked and kept moist by a gentle spray of water.

The seasons display themselves blatantly in Sicilian markets. Spring means artichokes, small, tight, purplish ones that can be bought ready-cooked, along with boiled potatoes, for a quick, hunger-appeasing snack. It's also the season for broad beans, to be eaten raw or cooked, sometimes combined with the artichokes, and for the long, pale green *zucche*, a kind of squash that could have stepped straight out of a medieval illumination. Tomatoes are there, of a hue which would seem unripe and unnatural in an Australian spring but which here are sweet and flavoursome. Fruits, too, announce the season: blood oranges with their crimson flesh (which yield juice of a most disconcerting appearance); tiny, delicate wild strawberries (*fragoline*) and the much larger fruit of commercial cultivation; and piles of orange loquats.

Most emblematic of the season, however, are the meats. In the week before Easter the market is stocked with baby lambs and kids for the Easter feast. (Curiously, the lamb is called *pecorella* in Sicily, an old-fashioned diminutive of the Italian for sheep, *pecora*, rather than the usual *agnello*, and the older hogget is known as *castrato*, a term which has survived since the medieval era.) Whole, except for their inner workings, they hang in rows outside the butchers' shops and stalls, stiff-limbed in their fleecy or hairy coats, with a wooden skewer running from one side of the ribs to the other. I would like to see a Palermo signora buy one, just to discover how it could be wrapped or parcelled for the trip to the kitchen, but perhaps it was still too early in the week. Heads are sold separately. The sight of four furry, unbloodied heads on an ancient wooden block, behind the simple sign '*Testa*', immediately sent my mind back to a fourteenth-century illustration, reminding me that eating habits are perhaps the most enduring of all.

I have further cause to ponder the endurance of traditions when, on Easter Sunday, driving through the middle of Sicily, I am swept into a swarm of traffic leaving the town and heading for the country. An earthquake, perhaps? Nothing so dramatic. On this fine, warm, sunny holiday city dwellers are off to visit friends and relations in the country, and they are being welcomed with a simple, country ... barbecue! I smell it as I drive past the paddocks of prickly pear, all in neat rows, and the brilliant green expanses of wheat. The houses are not too far from the road, and I can see how everything is prepared for the arrival of guests: long, family-size tables set outside, in the shade of a tree, and covered with plastic cloths. The fire is glowing, and suspended above it is the lamb – not just chops sawn indiscriminately from the nearest part of the carcase, but a whole animal, shiny with oil and gently sizzling to gleaming doneness.

And of course I remember the lamb-less flocks I had seen grazing here and there, under the olive trees, amongst the vines. I remember the baskets of fresh ricotta being delivered, still dripping, to the *salumeria*. I remember watching the women in the *pasticceria* almost in a production line, packing and gift-wrapping Easter *cassata* in delicate shades of pale pistachio green and ivory. And suddenly, it all made sense: the sheep, which are as much a feature of the landscape as the olive trees, provide both the lamb and the milk, which is transformed into ricotta, which in turn becomes the base of the cassata. The cassata, too, is of ancient tradition; the extravagant decoration of glazed pears and oranges surrounded by loops of *zuccata* hints at its Arab ancestry. The *zuccata* itself, a sweet, sticky paste made from the marrow-like *zucca*, goes back at least as far as the fourteenth century, recorded in a recipe of the Catalan *Sent Sovi*. And the marzipan lambs? Marzipan, too, came to Sicily with the Arabs, though it is still known by its Catalan name, *pasta reale*.

In this environment, everything fell into place. The religious association was no more than the sanctioning of the traditional agricultural rhythm, so that the products of the season had been imbued with a symbolic significance. It was a perfect example of the integration of Nature and Culture.

MEDITERRANEAN INSPIRATION

*One minute you will be passing through the traditional
Mediterranean polyculture — olives, vines, figs and artichokes,
in the distance the shepherd with his flock of sheep — and the
next minute, on the other side of the rise, your eyes will be hit by
the shimmering glare of hectares of plastic, the face of modern
agribusiness, forcing the growth of earlier-than-early beans and
richly coloured but tasteless strawberries.*

WHEN THE SKY BLUE-RINSES itself and raises itself from its winter
torpor, when the sweet fragrance of orange blossom greets me as
I step outdoors, and when the warmth of the sun reaches my very

marrow, then my inspiration turns, almost by instinct, to the Mediterranean. I forget about thick soups and sturdy pies, and stock my shelves with black, green and wrinkled olives, with firm, pink-and-white, peppercorn-studded salami, fresh pecorino cheese, chick peas and tahini and other Mediterranean staples. I ignore potatoes and look for rice to accompany my lemony grilled chicken. I pass over beef in favour of lamb, while it's still young enough to be called lamb, and I harvest herbs and greens from the garden for my salads.

As the season progresses to its harsh, inhuman peak, my enthusiasm for the sun begins to pale, but the Mediterranean still guides my cooking and eating. I grill *cevapcici* and *merguez* and lamb perfumed with the Moroccan mixture of spices known as *ras-el-hanout*, and lunch on the Greek salad of tomatoes, cucumber, feta and olives that was our standard midday meal in Kalamata. Hot nights are made bearable by a Spanish *gazpacho* which also takes care of a tomato surplus. And *pastis*, milky white and aniseedy, comes into its own.

Taking another cue from the Mediterranean, the time to dine is not when the clock says so but when it feels right, when the stark daytime glare has softened into a languid evening haze and the rim of the sun beyond the horizon turns the sea as wine-dark as Homer described it. Once body and soul have relaxed with the waves' gentle massage and are at one with the universe, then is it time to dine.

What is the Mediterranean? It is a climatic unity, a linguistic, agricultural, historical, gastronomic unity. It is grape vines and olives and Roman red roofs. In France, it's the Midi, said to begin at Lyons, a town precariously situated on the *oc-oil* linguistic frontier which separates the South from the North. In his classic *The Food of France*, Waverley Root wrote that for him, descending from the north, the Midi began a little further south, at Montélimar (famous for its nougat). But even before that, after you escape from the smoke and stench of industrial suburbia in the imperceptible merging of Lyons with Vienne, and pass beyond Vienne, you are suddenly aware that the sky is clearer and bluer, the clouds are untouchably high, and friendly plane trees on either side of the road welcome you. As your eyes awaken to a landscape of vineyards and espaliered pear and apricot trees, you discover again the pleasure of breathing. You observe that life seems rosier in the Midi, and wonder how and why you could ever have been induced to leave.

It's not just because the climate tells me so that I lean towards the foods and cuisine of the Mediterranean, but because I feel empathy and fascination for that uniquely focused, self-contained part of the globe. As the home of the Gods, it is familiar through literature; its languages are familiar through years of study; but most of all, its familiarity derives from its similarities to Australia.

Was it the scent in the air that made me feel 'at home' the minute I stepped off the train at Nice one balmy spring evening? Or was it that I had unconsciously absorbed the culture, so that this 'foreign' country was in no way foreign? There are so many hints of 'home' in the Mediterranean – roads lined with oleanders in southern Italy and with gum trees in Barcelona, clumps of eucalypts and golden-blossoming wattles in Sicily, a peppercorn tree in Morocco that immediately took me back to a swing in a dusty outback schoolyard. There is the parched summer landscape, and the proximity of the sea – or at least, the knowledge that it is there – and above all, the sky, so high, so sharply blue.

Even the fish of the sea are familiar, gleaming silver or rosy pink, unlike the pale, flat, unnatural aberrations of colder Atlantic waters. Exploring the fish market at Sète, in the company of Alan Davidson's *Mediterranean Seafood*, I found the fish of my childhood (and a few others) – snapper, poddy mullet, 'rainbow' fish striped in pink-green-blue (officially, rainbow wrasse), rockcod (the esteemed *rascasse*), tailor, the 'sergeant baker', mulloway . . . and octopus.

Octopus, and squid, are quintessentially Mediterranean. The ancient civilisations of Crete and Mycenae decorated their pottery vases and urns with the most endearing octopus and squid, and mosaic floors in Roman villas included octopus and squid in their galaxies of marine life. In my childhood, octopus was simply food for fish. You caught it with a length of wire bent into a hook at one end, with a strip of white singlet trailing to lure the octopus from under its cosy rocky ledge. Later, I learnt that it was edible, delicious, and prized by people of the Mediterranean. In Corfu once, on a clear and cloudless night, I went out in a shallow-bottomed boat in quest of squid and octopus. The squid meandered, semi-transparent, near the water's surface, while the octopus sprawled indolently on the sea floor, but neither was quick enough for the fisherman's spear, which struck with deadly accuracy.

These wide wooden boats were rowed from the bow, standing and facing forward – which made good practical sense, since you could see what lay ahead. This was directly opposite from the way I had been used to rowing, seated in the middle of the boat and heading backwards. Until then, I hadn't imagined that a boat could be rowed any differently, but later I noticed in other parts of the Mediterranean, and in old paintings, that boats were always rowed frontwards. Back in Australia, I realised that the Italian fisherman at Norah Head rowed in that very same way when he checked his lobster pots on the edge of the reef.

This timelessness is one of the great fascinations of the Mediterranean. It is reassuring to know that Saturday is still *jour de marché* in Pézenas, as it has been for the past six or seven hundred years; that my Italian butcher prepares his *prosciutto* in the same way as prescribed by the first-century Roman writer on agriculture, Columella; that Italian *pasticcerie* still sell miniature sweets called *cannelle*. These tiny shreds of cinnamon-bark, thickly encrusted with sugar, recall the sugared spices customarily offered at the end of a medieval dinner for the purpose of helping digestion – and in Italy you can find other toffee-like sweets flavoured with bitter herbs and known as *digestivi*. It is heart-warming to recognise in a recipe a Dalmatian cousin gives me ('this is what we do with fish when we catch too many') a dish known to the Roman gourmet Apicius – essentially, fried fish dressed with a vinegary sauce and eaten cold, or at room temperature. This same elementary technique is used by Catalans for their *escabetx de peix*, by Sicilians for their *sarde a scabece*.

I find it moving that the chestnut-roasting pan used by friends in the Languedoc, with its round perforated bottom, is exactly as described in a fourteenth-century Provençal inventory – as is their iron grid, on short, stubby legs, which grills coils of sausage over *sarments* (dried vine prunings) in their enormous fireplace. I am excited to discover that the *maccu* that I eat in Palermo – a drab beige puree in a wide, shallow soup bowl, relieved only by a spiral of green-gold olive oil – is the *minestra de fave*, puree of broad beans, for which I have seen recipes in medieval manuscripts, and which is certainly of far more ancient origin. I get a thrill recognising, in the *civet de lapin*

•

•

which Fifine demonstrates for me and which is thickened with mashed liver, a medieval Catalan antecedent. I enjoy recognising traces of popular Latin in local variants – *castrato* in Sicily, for mutton; *ventrèche*, in southern France, for the salted belly pork known as *pancetta* in Italy; *la masse*, for a kind of wooden pestle used to tamp down the just-picked grapes in their big wooden tubs before being transported to the *cave*; and *colh*, the name given in the Languedoc to a team of grape-pickers.

It is gratifying, too, to note the respect accorded Nature and the willingness of commerce and bureaucracy to bow to her exigencies. Since wine is the life-blood of the Languedoc – cars carry bumper stickers with the slogan *Buvez du vin!* (Drink wine!) – the rhythm of life changes when it is decreed that the grapes are ready for the *vendange*, the grape harvest. The bakery bakes more bread and the butcher offers his meat and charcuterie seven days a week. Schools open their doors early and arrange for a hot midday meal for children who would normally go home to eat. No one ever gets married during the *vendange*, and for anyone unlucky enough to die, the usual at-home ceremony and funeral procession are done away with. The local council offers its *salle des fêtes* to the group of Spanish grape pickers for a Saturday night celebration. *La vendange* involves the whole community.

Such long-standing customs are typical of cultures in which religion and folk tradition are integrated into a coherent whole. In some Sicilian churches, primitive *ex votos* express gratitude for cures of all manner of worldly ills. Notre-Dame-de-la-Garde in Marseille, high on a windy hill overlooking the port, is festooned with ships of all shapes and sizes representing thanks for prayers answered and sailors returned. The Provençal *crèche* displayed every Christmas shows the

•

•

infant Jesus in a stable – in the middle of a typical Provençal village. Bearing gifts for the newborn are the traditional *santons* in traditional dress: the old women with baskets of thyme and lavender, with garlands of garlic, trays of figs, urns of oil, bundles of twigs, together with the fisherman with his box of fish, the baker in his floury apron, the shepherd carrying a lamb across his shoulders, the old man with the Yule log, the *bûche de Noel*. Each character has its place in everyday reality. Sicilian crèches are similarly peopled with the characters of Sicilian life – the fish merchant with three red mullet and an octopus in his basket, the old peasant lady carrying a wicker tray of prickly pear fruit – but also include a touch of hyperreality in the out-size and glittery Christmas star somehow suspended above the grotto where the sheep and donkeys and baby are forever fixed.

Mediterranean cultures are characterised by a contiguity of myth and reality, naivete and ingenuity, crudeness and sophistication. At Aci Trezza, on the rocky eastern coast of Sicily, you can still see the huge volcanic rocks hurled by the Cyclops when his eye was pierced. In Greece, on the way to Delphi, you pass the crossroads where Oedipus met his father. Spanish churches, which seem to make a feature of gaudy and bloody representations of a headless John the Baptist (often carrying his head on a platter), are likely to be decorated with boughs of soft white almond blossom in February. The gaily decorated horse-drawn carts of Sicily have all but disappeared, but the tradition has transferred itself, quite naturally, to the small trucks which carry the produce of orchards and gardens to market.

The landscape can also illustrate a paradox. One minute you will be passing through the traditional Mediterranean polyculture – olives, vines, figs and artichokes, in the distance the shepherd with his flock of sheep – and the next minute, on the other side of the rise, your eyes will be hit by the shimmering glare of hectares of plastic, the face of modern agribusiness, forcing the growth of earlier-than-early beans and richly coloured but tasteless strawberries.

But the past continues to exist in the present. The features that distinguished Mediterranean diet in the medieval centuries – before the arrival of tomatoes and peppers, beans and potatoes – are still, by and large, valid. Bread was by preference made from wheat, rather than rye, barley or mixed grains, and lamb and kid were the favoured meats. There was plenty of wine and olive oil, but little in the way of milk or butter. Pork and fish were dry-salted to make prosciutto and anchovies. People ate more vegetables, and a greater variety of them than in the north. The standard treatment for fresh fish and squid was frying, the standard accompaniment a wedge of lemon or bitter orange. Sauces were more varied, more imaginative, than in northern regions, and often thickened with almonds, walnuts or hazelnuts. Sugar was used with discretion. These are the elements of which the gastronomic unity of the Mediterranean is composed.

Cookbook author Diane Seed has represented the typical Mediterranean diet as '*cucina povera*', the food of the poor, based on the classical trilogy of wheat, wine and olives enhanced with vegetables, herbs, spices and garlic. The three staples are treated with reverence; bread is baked in fanciful and often allegorical forms for age-old rituals. In Sicily, once known as the granary of Italy, bread is never wasted. As crumbs, it enters into countless dishes, from pasta to meat and fish. Some of the best bread I have ever eaten came from the Spinnato *panificio* in Palermo.

Mediterranean cuisine is similarly represented as *artisanale*, more natural than formalised French cuisine. Linked to the land and its seasons, it is perceived as uncorrupted by industrialisation. One May Day in Rome I ate crisp-fried artichokes – *carciofi alla giudea* – in a little restaurant near the Campo de' Fiori and a few days later, in the hills outside the city, fresh broad beans with mature pecorino. Humble foods indeed, but in the context of today's values they assume the character of cultural super-foods.

The wholesome, homely qualities associated with Mediterranean foods have been grafted to the generic 'Mediterranean diet'. Synthesised by nutritional experts and elevated to cult status, this is the diet being promoted to today's health-conscious (and typically non-poor) yuppies. Along with the oyster, the Mediterranean diet offers a rare example of upward mobility in the food world. Usually the trend is in the reverse direction, the lower classes adopting the foods and eating habits of their social superiors. The very Mediterranean blend of naturalness, primitiveness and tradition has endeared the new 'Mediterranean diet' to a generation of nostalgia-seeking post-modernists who also value the antiquity of its culture and cuisine.

Other countries, other regions might have similarly enduring cuisines and traditions, but in none other is wine so intricately integrated or symbolically significant – or so economically important. In the local paper of the Languedoc, the *Midi-Libre*, prices on the Béziers wine exchange for red and white wines, according to their alcoholic percentage, are quoted daily. Even the Persians and Arabs enjoyed wine in pre-Mohammed days. Mediterranean food without wine is unthinkable.

This is one reason I feel a natural affinity for the foods of the Mediterranean. But also, I enjoy their flavours for what they are, and

●

●

for what they represent. Perhaps I am being impractically over-romantic when I imagine I am absorbing a whisper of Mediterranean-Arab culture when I stuff peppers with rice and currants and pine nuts, or when I prepare a meat-and-vegetable stew with the ritual seven vegetables as an accompaniment to couscous. Perhaps it is ridiculously idealistic to conceive the Mediterranean as a kind of primitive paradise, an escape from the machinations of the modern world. Too bad; I prefer to stay with the myths.

THE ART OF CUISINE

---

*Cookery is not chemistry. It is an art. It requires
instinct and taste rather than exact
measurements.* — Marcel Boulestin

CUISINE IS TO INGREDIENTS what language is to words.

Ingredients and words can each have an independent existence, randomly scattered throughout the universe, but when they are brought together with conscious purpose the effect is exponentially greater. Think of 'I', and 'am', and the infinitely more powerful 'I am'; or egg yolk, and oil, and the miraculous mayonnaise. With the contribution of culture – in other words, human intervention – these

•

•

separate entities are combined and transformed into expressions of far greater complexity and eloquence.

A Frenchman encountered in a Parisian wine bar, L'Ecluse, once explained to me, *'Mais le poisson grillé, ça, ce n'est pas la cuisine. La cuisine, ça se prépare.'* ('Grilled fish is not cuisine. Cuisine is something that requires preparation.') And this preparation, he implied, included thinking about the initial ingredients and the final dish, and the means of getting from the former to the latter. This is the vital cultural component, reflected also in the overheard remark of a woman to her friend, as foil-wrapped packages of barramundi were placed on the hotplate for a do-it-yourself dinner at a Kakadu resort, 'That's not cooking. That's throw-it-on-and-let-it-do-itself.'

Perhaps this fundamental analogy is what inspired structuralists such as Claude Lévi-Strauss and Mary Douglas to argue that cuisine *is* a language – and insofar as it is a means of communication, a conveyor of symbolic meaning, cuisine is without doubt a language, though surely that is a secondary function, not its raison d'être. How many cooks talk through their food, and consumers understand?

Much debate on the nature of cuisine centres on whether it is art or craft. According to many definitions, both are skills but art seems to be differentiated on the basis of the aesthetic qualities of the finished product. Craft can produce things of beauty, too, though crafts are not required to have aesthetic qualities and are not necessarily judged by such criteria. In one of programs of the Thames Television series 'Take Six Cooks', the chef Raymond Blanc made an impassioned plea for the recognition of cuisine as art. 'Why shouldn't a chef, at the peak of his career, be considered an artist, like any creative craftsman?'

The cry is as old as cuisine itself. In the early years of the fifteenth

•

•

century Maistre Chiquart, chief cook to the court of Savoy, claimed an artistic side to cuisine; similarly Carême, the most celebrated French chef of the early nineteenth century, argued valiantly for the inclusion of patisserie, as a branch of sculpture, among the fine arts. Brillat-Savarin wrote, 'Cooking is the oldest of the arts.' Yet the controversy continually resurfaces. Raymond Blanc's question was, in a sense, rhetorical – but the mere fact of its asking implies that typically, cuisine is not considered an art, nor its practitioners artists.

Like any art, cuisine involves a considered choice – among ingredients, methods of preparation and cooking and manners of presentation, with a certain end in view and with due respect for the ultimate fate of the final product, which is to be eaten. All artists go through this process. A sculptor will choose the material, the tools, to realise a certain vision. Whether the end result is art or just a funny lump of rock will depend on the craftsmanship or mastery of skills, together with the imaginative vision of its creator and the aesthetic impact, which itself depends on the values of the society. The culinary work of art must additionally engage and excite the sense of taste. Technical perfection might produce admiration, but without the imagination and inspiration, it cannot be called art.

If I hadn't already been convinced of this, I would have been persuaded by a salad that combined grilled prawns dressed with 'pesto oil' (essentially, a blend of pureed basil and olive oil) with a stack of roasted red peppers and thin slices of 'honey glazed eggplant', the whole scattered with lightly toasted pinenuts for good measure. There was a minor quibble that neither the eggplant, nor the peppers, nor the basil were exactly seasonal at the end of winter – though this was Australia, with such varied climatic zones and such rapid transport that seasonality can become meaningless. The prawns were as moist and tasty as you might have expected for that kind of prawn, the peppers nicely roasted, and the presentation attractive, but there was no vision, no unifying principle, neither theoretical nor gustatory. There was no way of understanding this dish in a historical or cultural context, nor were there intellectual or sensory clues in the association of ingredients. It was an amalgam of diverse elements that emphatically did not come together as a whole, a supreme example of unnecessary accessorising. The scattering of pinenuts was gratuitous, as were the odd leaves of rocket sandwiched between the eggplant and red pepper segments. The effect was like that of a room painted with walls of red, yellow, orange and violet.

Technical skills can be acquired, but the artistic vision comes from the soul, from the individual's imagination. Artist-cooks, Raymond Blanc's creative craftsmen, need a degree of liberty and freedom from the restraints imposed by budgets or bosses, together with the understanding and encouragement of patrons. For these reasons they are more likely to be found in the realm of haute cuisine than in the humble hamburger joint. According to author Jean-François Revel, invention, renewal and experimentation are the hallmarks of an 'erudite' cuisine, the province of professional chefs with the knowledge, time and resources to create and innovate. In Revel's terminology, erudite cuisine represents one extreme of the culinary system. At the other is popular cuisine, stable, intimately linked to the land and its resources.

It has sometimes been argued that cuisine advances through technological innovations – though when you think about it seriously, it's hard to name any culinary innovations and advances that have been introduced by technology. Not since Prometheus stole the fire for us – and that *did* spark a gastronomic revolution – has there been any invention to divert the course of culinary evolution. In recent years, technology has produced the Mixmaster and the Magimix, both of which offer economies of time and labour but haven't really initiated any evolutionary leap forward. They might have democratised the gâteau, the mousseline and the julienne – levelled the playing field, in the current jargon – but this hardly equates to progress. The introduction of sous-vide cooking, in a vacuum-sealed plastic bag, merely promises benefits for supermarkets and caterers. Even the advent of refrigeration, about a hundred years ago, did very little for the state of the culinary art. Jellies suddenly suffered a vogue at the start of the twentieth century, but jellies had been around for seven centuries or more.

What technology has achieved is to liberate cuisine so that the art of the cook today is seen less in mastery of technique than in control over ingredients. Which helps explain why so much attention is now given to the choice of raw materials, their source and authenticity, and to the combination of flavours. If achieving the perfect texture of a prawn quenelle requires no more skill than measuring ingredients and counting the seconds in the food processor, then the arena for originality becomes mastery of flavour and flavour individuality.

The transformation of the chef from artisan to artist is often credited to the magic wand of the French Revolution, which transformed Paris into a city of restaurants (though restaurants actually began to proliferate *before* the Revolution). Restaurants were democratic eating places that welcomed anyone with an adequate purse, and they offered the chef simultaneously independence, artistic licence and a vastly increased audience. This implies that artist status is dependent on public recognition. The same might be true of an author. A work, whether a book, a painting or a new dish, is created and subsequently consumed in an act as private and individual as the creation. Public recognition comes when the work is talked about, reviewed, discussed in the press – which requires, and presupposes, educated consumers. But chefs need immediate recognition; their creations cannot be hoarded in dusty drawers in the hope of discovery by great-grand-children. Contemporary appreciation and approval, however, usually mean conformity with ruling fashions, which in turn impose their own restraints. Fame more enduring might be achieved through publishing books of recipes, or of memoirs, though this means calling on the literary system for support, and taking the risk that reproduction of the recipes by less talented hands might result in something less than art.

Most works of art can be conserved and reproduced, secure in the knowledge that the original still exists. Not so with cuisine, ephemeral in essence, though as with performance art its creation can be recorded on camera so that the step-by-step production and final product can be fixed forever on film. But visual media, however well they work for theatre or dance, cannot capture the flavour, the aroma, the texture which are as much a part of the culinary art as its façade. This is what thwarts those cooks who would be – indeed, who are – artists, for so long as the accepted criteria for a work of art cannot cope with a product that is neither permanent nor able to be cap-tured in some form or other, then cuisine seems destined to remain an also-ran in the artistic stakes.

To argue that cuisine ought be recognised as an art is not to deny that it is also a craft. There is a repetitive aspect to craft, reproducing the same thing, or variations on the same thing, over and over, and all cooks and chefs and artists are craftsmen in some degree – consider Picasso's prodigious output of ceramics during his stay at Vallauris. Raymond Blanc's plea was for the recognition of the chef as creative craftsman. Because cuisine is simultaneously art and craft, involving vision and skill, it is as much a cultural activity as writing or sculpting. Like these, cuisine is both practice and product, the process of creation and the creations themselves – the art of cuisine and cuisine as art.

RECIPES AND RIGHTS

'How many stars did you give Chrysanthème?'
'Three. I was sticking to two over the gâteau de crabe,
but I capitulated to his kidney beans with caviar sauce.'
'Kidney beans and caviar. Now that is elegant!'
'Treat cheapies as if they're jewels, and precious stuff as if it's
nothing. Very Chanel food.' – Francine du Plessix Gray

FLICKING THROUGH A BOOK for microwave cooks recently, I
noticed a recipe entitled Pastry Swirl with French Almond Cream.
Actually, I noticed the full-page, full-colour photo first, and recognised it – even with the strawberry in the centre – as a *gâteau Pithiviers*:

•

•

scallop-edged circles of puff pastry enclosing a rich, sweet, almond filling, the surface glazed and decorated with the customary spiral of knife-etched swirls.

From the given name I would never have known that the recipe has a long and honourable ancestry, dating from about the seventeenth century and the reign of La Varenne; nor that the pastry is a speciality of the Loire town of Pithiviers, an hour or so south of Paris. Naturally, there's no copyright attached to a tradition, no intellectual property rights. Anyone can take any one of a multitude of 'authentic' recipes for *Pithiviers*, modify it, rename it and present it as new. Who cares, as long as it tastes good? Well, I do, for one. I believe the cultural context is also important, and since I'm familiar with the story of the Pithiviers, a slice of something labelled *Pithiviers* would taste different (to me) from a slice of Pastry Swirl with French Almond Cream.

Sometimes there is good reason for renaming a recipe, as when the name of a dish in its own language is utterly unpronounceable by outsiders (if they can read it!). Or when there's simply no equivalent in the other language, so that the name substituted describes the composition of the dish. There's no translation for *Pithiviers*, but it would have been more honest to call the recipe Pithiviers cake – following the model of Banbury cakes and Chelsea buns. Alternatively, if there's to be an explanatory description (Pastry Swirl with . . .), this should be appended to the proper name, like a sub-title in a foreign film, which is what most Thai and Chinese restaurants do. But sometimes, just occasionally, the renaming reflects the devious intent of concealing the true origins of a recipe 'lifted' unceremoniously from somewhere else – though most recipe writers today are extremely conscientious and take care to include proper attributes. (Indeed, sometimes too much

•

•

care. It's useful to know that this particular recipe represents someone's approximation of a dish eaten in the Great Mongolian Desert but the formality can be taken to extremes; there's a naively precious air to cookbooks in which every second recipe came from 'my special friend' and 'my dear colleague'. Where did the friends and colleagues get their recipes?)

Every dish has a story. Even if I just invented it by throwing together, with judicious timing, the resources of refrigerator and pantry, it has its story. That it will never be replicated is of no consequence. There are other dishes that are being, have been, and will be reproduced, and in whatever culture they have their home they are called traditional. They have a name. Renaming such dishes is tantamount to denying their stories, and appropriation of a recipe with total disregard for its story shows a lack of respect for tradition.

Appropriating a name and applying it to a different dish is also cocking a snook at tradition – which is exactly what many of the nouvelle cuisine chefs did in the 1970s, deliberately subverting convention and mocking the rules and rigour surrounding a particular recipe. In gentle jest they turned the language topsy-turvy, so that '*darne*' no longer referred to a cut of salmon, nor '*escalope*' to a slice of veal. Ignoring exclusive rights of names to dishes they irreverently composed a terrine of seafood as easily as their predecessors made one with pork, a compôte of stewed rabbit rather than stewed apple, a soup based on strawberries instead of shellfish. These were radical breaks with tradition but, like the feminist bra-burning of the same era, they were necessary if barriers to progress were to be lifted.

Often, and especially in the hands of camp followers, the anarchy espoused by nouvelle cuisine has been exploited, creating a potential for confusion and embarrassment in restaurants which play with words as much as with ingredients. How can you understand menu items like coriander pesto, or sun-dried tomato pesto, when pesto has only ever meant a puree of basil, pinenuts, garlic, parmesan and olive oil? If *carpaccio* has previously been defined as paper-thin raw beef, dressed with oil and lemon juice and topped with shavings of parmesan, how to comprehend a *carpaccio* of tuna? You can ascribe such innovations to post-modern eclecticism or Dadaist free associations of ideas and ingredients, but if any sort of paste can be called a pesto, where is the respect for tradition?

Tradition is something passed from generation to generation. Traditional means time-honoured, with time the critical factor – though the time it takes to honour a dish can be as short as a few decades. And what is honoured in a dish is usually the idea, the concept, rather than the composition or the method. Fifty different cooks will produce fifty different versions of pesto, with more or less garlic, more or less basil, made by hand or made in a food processor. It's rare that tradition can be embodied in a single definitive recipe that claims authenticity.

'Authenticity' in food and cuisine – what it means, and whether and why it is relevant – is a matter of some controversy. On one side of the present debate are those who consider authenticity a noble virtue akin to honesty, an ideal that demands respect. On the other side of the table are those who regard it as a restraint on the chef's creativity and imagination, unnecessarily restrictive and totally irrelevant to today. They see the pro-authenticists as pedantic purists, while these in turn see the others as flippant mockers of tradition. It's a debate that contains echoes of another great controversy: the Ancients and Moderns debate of the seventeenth century. The Ancients upheld the primacy of classical antiquity, deeming the works of ancient Greece and Rome writers the very models of literacy excellence. The Moderns took their cue from Descartes (whose contributions to geometry had advanced the science of mathematics) and challenged this notion, arguing that if progress could occur in science then it was also possible in the arts. In this debate Cuisine seems to sided with the Moderns, La Varenne's *Le Cuisinier François* of 1651 formally inaugurating a new era of cooking on both sides of the Channel.

Authenticity, according to any dictionary definition, is the quality of being authentic – that is, reliable, trustworthy, genuine, true, certain, faithful, credible, official and authorised. There is a subtle distinction between authentic as genuine (opposed to spurious), and authentic as true (opposed to false). This latter interpretation presupposes the existence of an authenticating ideal, something to be true *to*, faithful *to* – such as the authentic manuscript. In French, '*authentique*' describes an item whose origin – its era, fabrication, source – is not in any doubt and, by extension, means that the item conforms to the model of the genre. When Proust wrote of quenelles that were authentic because they contained no '*alloy*', he meant that they respected to the letter the traditional formulation.

The authenticating ideal is a bit like the Holy Grail – it would clarify everything, if only you knew where it was. Not only is it illusory, but any attempts to define the authentic are invariably influenced by present-day values and standards and beliefs. And defining it, fixing it in a particular time and place, refuses it the room to move through history. Sometimes the authentic might be the original. For a dish like crème vichyssoise we can refer back to the recipe for this soup created by Louis Diat in America in the 1920s. Similarly, for carpaccio we need only go back some ten or twenty years to the Venetian chef who invented, or at least, discovered and popularised it. He named the dish in honour of the Venetian Renaissance painter Vittore Carpaccio, who favoured a certain shade of red in his work. Often, however, there simply isn't an original, or if there is it bears no relation to the contemporary version. Jugged hare began life in a real jug, but today the jug has no part in the recipe.

Pesto, in the eighteenth and nineteenth century, apparently referred to the meaty paste that might be used for filled pasta such as ravioli, or to an invalid dish of ground chicken mixed to a soupy puree with some of the broth. In either case, the name derived from the pounding of the ingredients, using a mortar and pestle. The basil-garlic-pinenut version of pesto, the form considered 'traditional' or 'authentic' today, was not baptised until the nineteenth century. It was not necessarily an *invention* of the nineteenth century, for sauces of herbs, nuts, garlic and oil had been made in Italy at least since Roman times and are almost certainly the ancestors of today's pesto. But these sauces doubtless evolved through many generations before the particular blend of basil, garlic and pinenuts, pounded together, was sanctioned with the name of 'pesto', the product of the pestle. And probably at the same time as it assumed this characteristic identity, previous 'pesto' preparations faded into obscurity and the basil pesto became the standard.

Tradition is typically seen as a vital ingredient, a guarantee of authenticity (though writer Frank Moorhouse has declared that, for him, authenticity resides not in traditionally prepared foods but in factory-made foods, such as canned spaghetti and asparagus, foods that fixed standards of flavour and appearance!). The assumption is that if a dish is true to tradition it must be authentic; reject tradition and authenticity flies out the window. So long as this recognises that tradition is not immutable, it is a valid premise. A romantic view sees tradition as tied to Mother Earth by an umbilical cord, and authenticity necessarily associated with salt-of-the-earth peasant origins. It's true that many traditional dishes are built from, and indeed dependent on, local resources but this is far from being a necessary condition, nor does reliance on the local produce automatically confer authenticity. There are many examples of traditional dishes which are not based on home-grown ingredients. *Brandade de morue* is traditional in the south of France, but the vital ingredient of salt cod comes from the north Atlantic. Plum pudding is traditional in England, but the dried raisins and currants and sultanas come from much warmer lands.

As the pesto example showed, traditions have a life of their own. So, too, cuisines. They evolve by incorporating new dishes, substituting new ingredients in old recipes, applying new techniques and new technology. New dishes might be born of culinary revolutions or of the meetings of two different cultures, as in the extraordinary interchange that followed the discovery of the New World when foods and cuisines crossed and recrossed the Atlantic. Wheat arrived in Mexico, and soon turned up in tortillas. Olives, introduced to Peru, were preserved by air-drying, using the same techniques as the locals had habitually applied to potatoes. In Columbia, the sugar from imported cane was combined with a local fruit, the guava, to supply the Spanish colonisers with a sweetmeat similar to *membrillo*, the quince paste that had been part of Spanish cuisine for centuries past. New traditions were born.

So when Italian pizza-makers in South America develop new versions of pizza to satisfy local tastes – pizza with pineapple, with plantains, with pineapple and gorgonzola – are not these further examples of cross-cultural hybridisation? They are a logical corollary of the basic pizza principle, bread dough plus topping, incorporating local ingredients, and their developmental history is essentially the same as that which produced wheaten tortillas and guava paste. If they survive beyond the novelty phase, they are on their way to becoming traditional.

But if a pineapple pizza can be legitimised in South America, why not in Australia a Satay Pork Pizza, the newest invention of a local pizza chain, 'with lashings of scrumptious toppings including special satay sauce, double mozzarella cheese, onion, capsicum, bacon, spicy pork and garnished with roasted peanuts'. Why not a 'Crustless Mexican Quiche', as featured in an American cooking class in 1984. Why not an parsley-and-pistachio pesto or a tomato-and-basil brie? Why not – as hypothetical examples of new tradition – a soy-and-ginger-flavoured mayonnaise, or Peking duck pasties? If flavour kicks are all that is wanted, then why not indeed?

Why not? My answer would be because they show no respect for tradition, no evidence of cultural integrity. Given the history of pesto, a parsley-and-pistachio variant sounds almost feasible, but there are no cultural links between southern Italy, where pizza is traditional, and South East Asia, where satays are traditional (and where the population is predominantly Muslim and abstains from pork), and certainly nothing that unites the two traditions in Australia. A quiche is a form of tart – the word itself means a sort of pastry – and a crustless quiche is inconceivable, especially when the Alsatian original is

•

7 4

•

lumbered with a Mexican filling. Brie is a cheese of northern France (in that country it is one of the 27 cheeses dignified with an '*Appellation d'Origine Contrôlée*' guarantee), while tomato-and-basil is synonymous with the Mediterranean. Mixing the two is like crossing sheep with goats.

Respect for its cultural associations should not straitjacket a dish or a recipe and deny it breathing space. Cuisines have to be able to grow, and the best way to grow seems to be as naturally as possible. New dishes are easily absorbed when they respect the cultural origins of ingredients and techniques. But if the innovation is a haphazard assemblage of diverse and unrelated elements, if it represents novelty for its own sake in a kind of gastronomic post-modernism, if it is a commercial attempt to 'diversify' merely for the sake of profit, then it should simply be allowed to live for the moment and die young. The cultural background should set limits to the flights of fancy, and respect for this should have precedence over empty-headed and narcissistic inventiveness.

The authenticity controversy is thus settled: creativity does not have to be incompatible with respect for tradition. And of course, there's flavour to be considered. Does any other pesto taste as good as the basil-garlic-pinenut one?

RUSSIAN MARKETS:

A FEAST FOR THE FEW

Communism is utterly incompatible with the production of food.
Communism might or might not have blood-red hands,
but it certainly does not have green thumbs.
— Henry R. Luce, editor-in-chief, *Time*

WHEN I VISITED RUSSIA in the summer of 1989 hearts still thrilled to the words *perestroika* and *glasnost*. The people I met and talked to – the harassed Intourist ladies, the enthusiastically patriotic tour guides, a leading industrial designer – were convinced that good

•

7 6

•

times were just around the corner. Today, they must seem as far away as ever.

A few years later, I heard a news report that life expectancy in Russia had decreased, a trend contrary to that in most developed countries. At the same time the incidence of alcoholism had increased, particularly among younger Russians who in other cultures might represent the affluent, post-war, baby-boomer generation.

If I lived in Moscow I don't doubt I'd be driven to drink, too. I remember studying the faces in the metro, at the time of openness and barrier-breaking inspired by Gorbachev, and being numbed by their emptiness and blankness, their uniform of impassivity. Even then these Muscovites appeared drained of any normal human aspiration beyond the need to survive – and for survival they would apply whatever cunning remained. These were people who would queue for, and accept with gratitude, foods most of us would reject on sight, such as devon-like sausage of the most artificial pink, manufactured to government specifications and sold in metre-long rolls. But they had no choice. There was one kind, and one kind only.

We see nothing remarkable in the variety – or pseudo-variety – that markets and supermarkets offer in western societies. Free markets, free enterprise, the benefits of competition, all of which underlie the functioning of our food system, are taken for granted. We forget that being able to choose what and how we eat is a luxury. Not that markets don't exist in Moscow and other Russian cities – they do. But the markets I visited were not democratic institutions of, by and for the people. They were for the few with power and money, acquired by whatever means.

Moscow's central market is the Tsentralnyi Rynok. Compared to the vastness of scale of most public buildings in the city, this one seemed almost human. What's more, it *smelled* like a market, appetising and irresistible. Emerging from the grandiose marbled caverns of the Moscow metro, I instinctively turned right, following my nose, and after a few metres I saw it. Or rather, I saw women coming and going, weighed down with shopping bags: unmistakable signs of a food market. Inside was a foyer with flower ladies and, beyond a short flight of stairs, the grand hall, with glorious displays of fruits and vegetables clamouring for attention. Beyond that again were a couple of small rooms leading to the outside, where a few independent stall-holders enjoyed the open air. This is where the mushroom man had his table. In early summer his offering was scant, with a few plastic bags of fungi resembling *girolles*, and an intriguing greyish-white growth that seemed more like a lump of coral. It looked totally unfamiliar, until I vaguely remembered specimens of Australian truffles preserved by the CSIRO. According to the mushroom man it is called (according to my interpretation of the cyrillic alphabet) '*baran*'.

Communication with the women at the market was practically nil, since my knowledge of Russian matched theirs of English. And the people behind the stalls were mostly women. Perhaps the wives go to market while the husbands take care of the cultivation side, for these quantities of fruits and vegetables must surely have come from an organised orchard and market garden industry rather than from someone's weekend dacha. Only the mushrooms, and the eggs and chickens in the meat hall – one dressed chicken and one bowl of speckled eggs for each sturdy, rosy-cheeked, kerchiefed babushka – may have represented cash-on-the-side from a backyard surplus or free forest pickings. Despite their kerchiefs and embroidered aprons these were not naive peasants but rather, keen-eyed and quick-fingered businesswomen.

In early summer there was a bounty of stone fruit – cherries of different kinds, several varieties of plums, peaches, apricots and golden loquats together with large, scarlet-fleshed watermelons, tiny misshapen apples and overflowing baskets of strawberries. Wild strawberries and blueberries, too, were sold in tall glass jars or simple paper cones. Later in the season I found other berry fruits, red currants, black currants and gooseberries, and the early apples and pears, typically small, irregularly shaped, but undeniably fresh.

On the opposite side were vegetables, similarly pristine and dewy fresh – the pink-and-white radishes, tight-furled lettuce and carrots with their tops. The tomatoes were reassuringly crimson and smelled like tomatoes ought to smell. But it was the herbs that won my heart, exquisitely fresh bunches of parsley, tarragon, chives, chervil, dill. In late summer the scent of dill pervades the whole market as it hangs in huge bunches, almost ready to flower. This is also the time of the cucumber glut, when the market will be full of small fat cucumbers ready to pickle, and the herb sellers offer ready-made faggots of pickling herbs (garlic, dill and vine leaf) as well as a kind of bouquet garni comprising slivers of carrot, parsnip and horseradish and a few stalks of parsley.

In another section of the market were the pickled vegetables, arrayed in white enamelled bowls, different types of pickled cucumber, whole green beans, tiny white squash and pickled heads of garlic – whole heads, which become almost translucent and take on a beautiful amber colour. In Russia it seems that any vegetable that can be pickled is so treated. Mushrooms are pickled with fresh herbs, bay leaves and spices such as peppercorns and cloves. Pickled red cabbage, pickled slivers of sweet red peppers, and a pickled spinach-like vegetable can turn up on your plate at almost any meal, and seem to be much more common than fresh vegetables.

Beyond the pickles were homely moulds of fresh cottage cheese, still imprinted with the weave of the cheesecloth and, next to them, bowls of curds ready to be drained. The fresh cheese will be made into breakfast fritters or served as is, perhaps with sugar or honey or fruit syrups or fruit preserves, in the Greek style. The honeys looked appealingly fresh and natural, some complete with the honeycomb. Each could be sampled before buying, and you buy only if you've taken your own container. This is not a profligate society, and used plastic bags have real commercial value.

Nothing was wasted in the meat hall, either – where at least you could see what you were getting, and know that it was real meat. Whole baby veal hung behind the counter, largish carcases of mutton and goat lay next to their heads, cleaned ready for the pot. Amongst the offal was a single pair of testicles – whose treat? On one table rested a charming quartet of baby sucking pigs (well, maybe not so baby), covered with a clean white sheet and tucked up as if for their afternoon nap.

This view from the market suggests that the Russians, with all these superb, fresh ingredients, must live in the best of all possible worlds. Russian markets, however, are never as busy as those in the streets of Paris, never as central to daily life as those of Asia, never as crowded as their state-run Gastronom food stores. Gastronom! With a name like that I expected a shop more entrancing than Fauchon, with floor-to-ceiling caviar, exquisite preserves made from mysterious dark berries and a bewildering display of smoked and salted fish. No one had told me that Gastronom was the Russian Franklin's, that there was one every few blocks, that almost none of them carried a complete range of ingredients, and that you'd have to be pretty desperate to find excitement in a floor display of packets of dehydrated eggs.

It's self-service, of a kind, at some Gastronom shops, but generally you go to different counters for different goods – sugar here, butter there, sausages somewhere else. Supermarkets, you begin to realise, have their advantages. In Russia patience is not so much a virtue as a prerequisite. Shopping demands infinite fortitude. Let's say you want to buy sugar. First you queue at the sugar counter, and when it's your turn you ask for six packets of sugar (you might as well buy six, it's no more arduous than buying one, and who knows when it will next be in stock?). Then, with your ticket, you queue at the KACCA, or cashier, and when it's your turn you pay and get a receipt. Finally, you return to the sugar counter and again wait your turn until, eventually, the woman hands over six packets of sugar, one at a time. You manage to get your arms around them and stagger to a nearby table that has been thoughtfully provided by the management to enable you to pack your purchases in the plastic bags you remembered to bring with you. Then you join the queue at the meat counter. At the Gastronom stores often the only meat was frozen and anonymous, though the pork was appealing, since Russian butchers apparently have not heard of new-fangled cuts, nor lean pork, and their chops had a healthy 3 cm of fat cover.

In the large cities, food was monotonous and standardised. Dangerous, too – no one cared about the large chunk of broken glass lurking at the bottom of my bowl of borsch. The menus might have been extensive, but most of the dishes were (shrug of the shoulders) unavailable. Forget about *stroganov* and *kulebiak, bliny* and caviar; these belong to the past.

The fate of many Russian artists and writers in the Stalinist period is now well documented. Russian cooking and eating traditions, it seems, have been similarly suppressed, or not allowed expression (though Stalin was perhaps not as inhuman as Ceaucescu, who reportedly did away with cookbooks in Romania). These are the very traditions which sustain a culture, in the same way as does religion. I only hope that the freedom and independence demanded by some of the states of the former USSR will extend to freedom of choice and the regaining of cultural and culinary traditions.

PUTTING CUISINE INTO
CULTURE

A cuisine is not shaped so much by its consumers as they, again in the most literal sense, are shaped by it. — Waverley Root

---

THE BUREAUCRACIES WHICH today administer and market Culture in Australia interpret it as 'the unique combination of the place where we live and the people'. Cultural resources are deemed to include 'anything that contributes to the culture of a particular place or people', and cultural life to be 'about participation, celebration, identity, belonging to a community and having a sense of place'. From this perspective, culture is a dynamic mix of people and resources, a process in which people are actively – and necessarily – engaged. Culture also concerns our identity as a nation, as a community, as individuals. According to the Australian cultural policy statement, *Creative Nation*, culture is fundamental to our understanding of who we are: 'culture is that which gives us a sense of ourselves'.

Nearly fifty years ago, in his book *Notes towards a definition of culture* (1948), T.S. Eliot similarly observed that to understand a culture is to understand a people. He insisted on 'an imaginative under-standing', for 'culture is not merely the sum of several activities, but a *way of life*' which includes 'all the characteristic activities and interests of a people: Derby Day, Henley Regatta, Cowes, the twelfth of August, a cup final, the dog races, the pin table, the dart board, Wensleydale cheese, boiled cabbage cut into sections, beetroot in vinegar, nine-teenth-century Gothic churches and the music of Elgar'. Make your own list, he suggested. What we eat, what we choose to eat, is implic-itly included. As Donald Horne wrote in *The Public Culture* (1986) a meat pie eaten in the street is part of the cultural 'language' of Melbourne, just as a raw herring eaten from a street stall in Amsterdam is part of its cultural 'language'. So eating Sydney rock oysters in a Sydney oyster bar is as much part of that city's culture as sipping a glass of champagne in Epernay. 'If we take culture seriously,' con-tinued Eliot, 'we see that a people does not need merely enough to eat (though even that is more than we seem able to ensure) but a proper and particular *cuisine.* One symptom of the decline of culture in Britain is indifference to the art of preparing food. Culture may even be described simply as that which makes life worth living.'

These interpretations welcome cuisine with open arms and take

•

8 4

•

it right into the heart of culture. For cuisine is more than just a basket of foodstuffs. It is what people do with those foods, the dishes that represent the product of ingredients and people's skills and ideas – and this applies equally to a tradition of pickled gherkins and the offerings of a high-class restaurant. Cuisine is just as much a medium for expressing culture as is art, literature, newspapers, television, architecture or urban design. If culture is 'one of the basic things which makes life worth living', as described in the South Australian arts and local government consultancy project, then it must include cuisine, which undoubtedly contributes – either for good or ill – to the quality of life of cities, towns and regions.

Cuisine can be a reflection of a region's identity, and at the same time lead the way in developing a community identity. While the Gourmet Weekends in the various Australian wine regions began as simply a blend of food, wine and tourism, they quickly attracted other 'cultural resources' and soon involved local musicians and artists as well. If we adopt Fernand Braudel's construction of cultural resources – namely, the multitude of material and spiritual goods representing religious values, art, ideology, intellectual developments and way of life – then recipes, the verbal record of cuisine, should be a cultural resource.

While cuisine is both practice and product, a medium of cultural expression and a consumable artefact produced by culture, it is the latter aspect that tends to dominate, such that a national or regional cuisine is usually described in terms of characteristic and customary dishes which in turn come to epitomise the culture. Alin Laubreaux had such an interpretation in mind when he wrote in *The Happy Glutton* (1931) that 'a cookery book will tell you more about the soul of a country than a whole row of Baedeckers'.

●

●

Like a soul, cuisine is not easily pinned down, defined and clari-
fied, nor can national cuisines be 'fixed' by identifying them with particular 'flavour principles'. In today's global village, such distinctions
lose their sharpness – and in any case, they cannot hope to comprehend the complexity of the different cuisines that coexist even within
the one 'national' cuisine as a result of social and regional affiliations.

The French gastronome Curnonsky recognised this when he
described the four distinctive types of cuisine to be found in France, all
part of its national cuisine. There was the *haute cuisine* of the top
chefs; the home-style *cuisine bourgeoise*; the specialities of regional
cuisines; and *cuisine paysanne*, peasant or impromptu cuisine, that
depends on whatever is in the larder. *Haute cuisine* is represented
by expensive, elaborate, labour-intensive dishes such as are today conceived in three-star restaurants, while *cuisine bourgeoise* is typified
by order and economy and regional cuisines by tradition and stability.
Thus the repertoire of dishes that represents French cuisine ranges
from Paul Bocuse's truffle soup and the celebratory family dinner of
roast lamb with beans, to the *cassoulet* of Castelnaudary and Breton
pancakes made with buckwheat flour – not forgetting, of course, the
fast food alternative of *steak-frites* from roadside vans.

What makes dishes such as these representative of French cuisine
is partly their reliance on French ingredients (truffles, *confit* of duck or
goose), but also the fact that they are claimed as 'ours' by the French
and recognised as 'theirs' by visitors. For the French, they are a way of
expressing who and what they are. Whether or not they are foods of
everyday consumption is irrelevant and, indeed, many dishes promoted as regional specialities – *bouillabaisse, boeuf bourguignon* –
belong to the festive table, the restaurant menu, the proudly patriotic

dinner offered to visitors from another region or country. What matters is their story, their significance, their symbolic value. These constitute the link to culture.

If culture can be represented in cuisine, so cuisine can be developed as an expression of culture. In recent years the sedate market town of Arnay-le-Duc in Burgundy has been assiduously creating for itself a gastronomic tradition that also serves to define and affirm a regional identity and establish a sense of community solidarity. On the strength of a rather inconclusive episode of the sixteenth-century religious wars that saw the traditional Catholics opposing the reformist Protestants on a nearby plain, it has formed a tenuous association with Henri IV, who at that time was fighting with the Protestant armies. Henri IV, also known as '*le Vert Galant*', ruled France from 1589 until 1610, when he was assassinated by a certain Ravaillac. According to popular myth, Henri IV had wished for all his citizens a 'chicken in the pot' every Sunday. In honour of this popular king (or on the pretext of honouring him) Arnay-le-Duc inaugurated in 1990 a new summer festival under the name of *La Fête Henri IV*, the climax of which was the *poule au pot* dinner for which all the town's restaurants, and a good many private homes, prepared and served chicken in the pot – boiled chicken with vegetables. At the same time a new cake (the *Vert Galant*) was created, also a new sweet (the *Bonbon Henri IV*), and a selected Burgundy wine was bottled for sale under the name *Ravaillac*. The dinner and the new dishes are now part of Arnay-le-Duc's cultural tradition.

Similarly in Spain, in the region – and ancient kingdom – of Aragon in the north-eastern corner of the country, a cake called the *Lanzon* has become a symbol of regional identity. For years the Franco

•

•

regime in Spain had suppressed regional affiliations, but the death of the dictator in 1975 cleared the way for changes in the political system. One of the most important of these was the move towards decentralisation and the creation of autonomous regions, a move which happened to coincide with strong social pressure for affirmation of regional identities. Catalonia, which had managed to retain its characteristic language, traditions and heritage was one of the first to make claims for autonomy, and to be recognised. In Aragon, on the other hand, regional identity was difficult to locate, let alone reconstruct. There was no local language, no particular ethnicity; even the regional costume and song had only been invented near the end of the eighteenth century.

On the other hand Aragon did, and does, have a regional cuisine – or at least, a number of dishes universally acknowledged as being typically Aragonese. And there was a certain acceptance of political intervention in culinary and gastronomic affairs, such as the post-war decree that on a specified day of the week diners must restrict themselves to a main course in restaurants, while paying for a multi-course meal. The difference in price went towards reconstruction of the country. On this gastronomic base was built a scheme to promote acknowledgment of a regional unity. In 1983 the regional government of Aragon announced a competition for a cake, or tart, or something from the domain of patisserie, to celebrate the region's *jour de fête*, 23 April, which was also the day of the Feast of Saint George. St George had been instituted as the protector of the kingdom of Aragon as early as the second century and eventually became its patron saint. The competition was won by a cake called the *Lanzon*, created by the pastrycooks' association: a rectangular, multi-layered cake topped

•

•

with chocolate renderings of one or more symbols – the shield of St George, the flag of the region, or the traditional scarf worn knotted around the neck.

As a cake, the *Lanzon* was hardly an innovation. Its ingredients – butter, sugar, sponge cake and liqueur – could have belonged anywhere. What particularised it were the decorations that symbolised Aragon, and its association with a day of local significance – not that there was anything about St George, his deeds and his history which made him specific to the Aragonese. Nonetheless, the cake which celebrated his alliance with the region was very quickly accepted and integrated into local tradition. There were two significant reasons for this. It was associated with an annual *jour de fête*, and in Aragon, as in many other cultures, there had always been special patisseries for special days in the calendar (like hot cross buns in England, cassata in Sicily, for Easter). Moreover, as a dessert the *Lanzon* was outside the meal proper, and so did not displace any other traditional element of the feast. Thus the *Lanzon* came to be a instant speciality, and its consumption the acknowledgment of belonging to a particular community, of celebrating a regional culture.

A similar story can be told of the Christmas plum pudding in Australia. Even those families which sensibly reject the hot roast turkey or chicken in favour of a seafood spread, or cold ham and salads, succumb to the Christmas pudding tradition. You can argue until you're blue in the face that hot (or even warm) plum pudding is climatically inappropriate in Australia, yet in December miniature plum puddings are instant sell-outs in restaurants. The cold Christmas pudding (set with gelatine) and the frozen Christmas pudding ice-cream are tributes to Australian ingenuity, combining respect for tradition with an understanding of the exigencies of summer, but they have not yet been able to depose the English-style pudding and all it represents.

These examples show the relevance of cuisine to culture. They also suggest that featuring local ingredients might count for less than the meaning and the symbolisation of the new dish: how and why the ingredients are put together, and the story this represents. There must also be some feeling of shared values and customs among the people, an incipient sense of belonging or wanting to belong. In helping to give the inhabitants of Arnay-le-Duc and Aragon a sense of themselves these new dishes earned a place in their respective cultures. The *Lanzon* was accepted as a local speciality because it represented a collective spirit and sustained a regional identity. The *Vert Galant*, with almost no distinguishing features apart from its link with Henri IV, secured its place in tradition through promoting the gastronomic reputation of the town. Perhaps the Christmas pudding represents a past we are not quite willing to discard.

Culture is 'the unique combination of the place where we live and the people'. Cuisine is the product of foods and people. However we choose to depict it – a list of dishes, a vibrancy of style in the kitchen – cuisine goes hand-in-glove with culture.

TOWARDS AN

AUSTRALIAN CUISINE

The poor days. Spaghetti, mincemeat, the cheap red, eating
all the bread and butter and asking for another basket
of bread . . . — Frank Moorhouse

FIFTEEN YEARS AGO we were all buying the books of the great chefs – Senderens, Vergé, Mosimann, Troisgros – and ranging them alongside our series of Elizabeth Davids, the classics by Jane Grigson, Claudia Roden and Julia Child, and a few Australian ones by Margaret Fulton and Charmaine Solomon. Today our shelves, and those of the bookshops, are stacked high with Australian cookbooks. Restaurant chefs such as Stephanie Alexander, Tony Bilson, Chris Manfield and Paul Merrony have all produced worthy cookbooks. There are books by Australian food columnists and cooking teachers, and by 'new' Australians reworking the culinary traditions of the countries of their birth. And all these books contain recipes written for Australian ingredients, Australian tastes and Australian lifestyles – though increasingly, they're also appealing to an international readership.

You might say that Australian cuisine has come of age. For several years now restaurant guides have included a 'Modern Australian' category – usually the largest – alongside Italian, Lebanese, Japanese and other nationalities. Less than a cuisine, in the usual sense of a list of characteristic dishes, 'Modern Australian' is a style, an enthusiastic romp through the world's favourite recipes. Its bywords are 'fresh' and 'seasonal', with lots of colour, lots of salads, lots of fresh vegetable and herb flavours plus a healthy dash of sweet chilli. Bold and undisciplined (in the sense of being free of disciplinary shackles), 'Modern Australian' ranges widely across the continent, gleefully gathering prawns and green papaya, kangaroo and kumara, snake beans and sorrel, then with imagination and time-honoured techniques producing dishes that belong nowhere else – certainly not in England, nor in America, and nowhere in Europe or Asia. Perhaps in twenty years we'll look back and unconsciously date such dishes as 'very nineties', but perhaps we'll also see them as evidence of a culinary maturity, proof that Australian cuisine, however it continues to evolve, is 'a complete organism, sturdy, ... and as natural to our country as the gumtree' – to borrow the words of author Marjorie Barnard, describing Australian literature some fifty years ago.

•

•

But what is Australian cuisine? After a month's meals in country motels and city pubs, a visiting Martian would probably go home convinced that pumpkin soup was a national dish. We don't have a repertoire of dishes that say what and who we are, a repertoire from which an Australian student staying with a family in Japan could select one or two and present them as examples of Australian cuisine, as a Japanese student in Australia might offer tempura and sushi. And what sort of cuisine are we talking about? 'Modern Australian' originated in restaurants, the innovative cuisine of experimental and imaginative chefs. Jean-François Revel would see it as an erudite cuisine, a form of *haute cuisine* to which popular cuisine, the foods of the masses, is the customary counterpoise. In the cycle of degeneration and renewal sketched by Revel, the erudite cuisine periodically returns to the popular for energy and inspiration. In 'Modern Australian', the stimulation and vitality come not from an indigenous popular style but from the diversity of the world's cuisines, many of which are now represented in this country.

Such cultural heterogeneity, however invigorating and beneficial, is a spanner in the works when it comes to defining or developing an Australian cuisine. We have to know what it means to be Australian before we can express ourselves through a gastronomic identity. And as this meaning has changed over two centuries, so have concepts of 'Australian' cuisine. In the rugged, bush-pioneering era there was a certain pride for white Australians in living off the land, exploiting natural resources such as kangaroos and bandicoots, pepper leaves and native currants. In 1968 the perfect Australian meal, for food writer Oscar Mendelsohn, was a singular blend of the ubiquitous international with the home-grown Australian: avocado oysters (an avocado half filled with oysters and dressed with lemon juice and pepper); poached fillets of flathead with caper sauce; roast turkey with walnut stuffing, baked potatoes and butter-fried baby marrows; rum omelette; Girgarre blue cheese. A personal choice, certainly, but while Australian in substance it succumbed in style to mainstream ordinariness. In response to Mendelsohn's selection a reader of the *Epicurean* contributed his own version of the ideal menu, this time featuring what he considered 'real Australian' foods: cod's roe with sliced cabbage; oyster soup; grilled fillet of steak; lamb or beef; mango or paw-paw; cheese.

It should, in theory, be possible to add a question or two to the periodic census asking householders to nominate dishes that are regularly eaten in their household. It would then be a simple matter to establish a list of dishes that Australians consider typically theirs, and to put forward this list as the basis of a national cuisine, or even to compile lists of dishes for regional cuisines. Such a task might have been feasible in Australia fifty or one hundred years ago when the nation, culturally, was fairly homogeneous (in 1947, 91 per cent of the population was born in Australia and less than 0.2 per cent was born in a non-English-speaking country). Recipe books published in the first half of the century feature the same range of dishes, with only slight departures from this standard miscellany. Whether the *Green and Gold* or the *Commonsense*, the *Presbyterian* or Lady Hackett's *Australian Household Guide*, you're likely to find recipes for rabbit pie, Irish stew, fricasseed fowl, bubble and squeak, macaroni cheese, stewed oysters, welsh rarebit, queen pudding, apple pie, sponge cake, gingerbread, quince jam and green tomato pickle. (Where are they now?) Today, multicultural Australia – nearly one-quarter born overseas, almost

•

•

two-thirds of these born in a non-Anglophone country – shares a vastly expanded catalogue of 'typical' dishes, from couscous to curry, spaghetti to spanakopita, quiche to barbecued quail. A city café can nonchalantly advertise, on its footpath sandwich-board, an ecumenical lunchtime selection of 'rolls, bagels, quiches, focaccias'.

National – or regional – cuisines can't be invented to order. Nor can they be discovered, captured, put in a cage and visited every Sunday. This is why contests for Australiana menus, or for Australia Day recipes, or indeed any attempts at national culinary symbolism for such occasions as the Chefs' Olympics, can produce only arbitrary, atypical oddities – such as a salad of smoked kangaroo with witlof leaves arranged to resemble the sails of the Sydney Opera House. In the right sort of environments, however, cuisines can be nurtured and encouraged to grow. As T.S. Eliot wrote, apropos regionalism in Britain: 'What is wanted is not to restore a vanished, or to revive a vanishing culture under modern conditions which make it impossible, but to grow a contemporary culture from the old roots'.

One of the way cuisines grow is by absorbing new ingredients. And in most culinary cultures, the way new ingredients become integrated is by way of familiar methods of preparation and familiar recipes. Consider polenta: when corn was brought to Europe, it came bereft of the 'foodways', the traditional preparation techniques that had accompanied it in the New World, where it was cooked with lime before being transformed into tortillas. What did the Europeans do but grind the corn, like wheat or any other grain, and turn it into a solid gruel by boiling it with water. (History doesn't record the name of the intrepid baker – for surely there was one – who regarded cornmeal as analogous to wheat flour and tried to turn it into bread.) Perhaps they added cheese to enliven the stodgy mush, as they dressed pasta with grated cheese. Then one day they cooked too much, discovered the next morning that it had set firm, and reheated it over the fire to invent grilled polenta. And subsequently they added sauces, or the juices from roasting meats. And so the polenta tradition was born. Imperceptibly, what began as novelties became customary, and melded with what went before.

A similar story can be told of sugar in Mediterranean cuisines, way back in the medieval era. When cane sugar was introduced by the Arabs it was initially recognised as a luxury replacement for the habitual sweeteners, honey and the richly flavoured syrup made by boiling down grape juice. Gradually sugar usurped their role, so that sweetmeats that had previously been made with fruits and honey began to be made with fruits and sugar. And probably a similar story can be told of chillies which, according to my theory, replaced the more expensive pepper and other spices in some Asian cuisines.

Analogous processes are at work in Australia where, contrarily, the 'new' ingredients are indigenous and it is the culinary traditions that are imported. One of the functions of cuisine is to take new ingredients under its wing so that we get to experience them in ways that we know and like. The French have a word for this: *apprivoiser*, which means, in a way, to domesticate, not so much like the dog that has the run of the house, but like the lorikeets that perch on the edge of the balcony for the morning crumbs. Cuisine socialises, so that the new ingredient becomes more familiar, the alien assimilated. Australia might not have a culinary tradition in the same way as Aragon or Burgundy, but there should be enough commonly recognised and accepted dishes for our indigenous ingredients – bush foods – to be allowed to sneak in under the coat-tails of a familiar patron and become one of the family.

We should not expect indigenous ingredients to go it alone, to be culinarily independent, creating their own contexts and proving their worth before they're accepted. We should be aiming for integration. Look what has happened with kangaroo, which now comes cured and smoked, marinated and herbed, char-grilled, roast, orientalised as a spicy rendang and stuffed into mettwurst. In fact, listing all the ways in which kangaroo has been *apprivoisé* gives a fascinating image of our multiculinary culture. Cuisine must be allowed to perform the socialising role it does so well, so that we happily welcome a lemon myrtle bavarois or a riberry bread and butter pudding the next time we meet them on a menu. While we don't have to focus all our gastronomic efforts on native ingredients, we do need to acknowledge, understand and use them. After all, suburban gardens accepted native plants years ago, with hardly an eyebrow raised.

If we are going to encourage an Australian cuisine to flourish, we have to let it grow from whatever roots have already been established, wherever they are and however tenuous and invisible some of them might be. It cannot be imposed, instantaneously created from a basket of approved ingredients. Adopting a purist approach and filling the basket with only indigenous ingredients would be as misguided as the 'ethnic cleansing' of national parks in which foreign intruders – self-sown blackberries and wild olives – are ripped out so that the native species can flourish. If we recognise the heterogeneity of the population, we should also recognise the heterogeneity of our food resources and include 'naturalised' foodstuffs – lamb, grapes, apples – as well as those foods which are unique to Australia. We must also recognise the heterogeneity of culinary traditions in a multicultural population. While we might learn from Aboriginal techniques, it is also appropriate to take inspiration from other cuisines. Brett Whiteley's art is no less Australian when it is consciously paying homage to Matisse.

We must also recognise that Australian cuisine has to say something about us, as Australians. It is not enough to take all-Australian ingredients and dress them in one of the culinary traditions represented in the country. A dish of Australian tuna prepared in a Mediterranean style – marinated in Australian olive oil with lemon juice and herbs, then grilled – might be theoretically justified as an example of Australian cuisine, but it cannot truly represent Australian cuisine until it is accepted in both restaurant and domestic kitchens, whether in Sydney or Port Lincoln or throughout the whole country. What we eat has to say who we are.

OPPORTUNITY LOST

Every country possesses, it seems, the sort of cuisine it deserves,
which is to say the sort of cuisine it is appreciative enough
to want. — Waverley Root

MARCUS CLARKE, author and journalist, fancied himself one of the few gastronomic connoisseurs of late nineteenth-century Australia, though his fluctuating fortunes meant his connoisseurship was infrequently exercised. Enthusiastically vaunting the 'Cafe Panard', a fictitious establishment modelled on one or other of the better restaurants of Melbourne in the 1880s, he commended its 'Soup of the clearest, red wine of colonial growth, but of fair flavour; an omelette, fried potatoes,

•

•

chicken and mushrooms, a salad dressed with oil and vinegar merely'. At this restaurant, he added, 'your soup is hot but without grease; your steak seems made for toothless gums; your salad bowl is filled with unbroken lettuce, and your coffee is as fragrant as the spice islands'.

While priding himself on his own good taste, he deplored the conduct of his countrymen who would 'vulgarise the place. They will begin by demanding beef and legs of bullocks, and get on to Yorkshire pudding, or perhaps roast pork and apple sauce. One monster – if you read this, sir, you will blush – after gobbling a perfect menu, asked when they were going to bring in the "solids". The solids! Another said audibly that – something his eyes – he would rather have a pot of porter and a raw onion with some bread and cheese than the whole blessed lot'.

Clarke himself was not unprejudiced. He simply thought French cuisine more elegant, refined and sophisticated than English cooking and looked down on those who did not share his preferences. While it was not uncommon in England to sneer at foreign – and 'foreign' almost invariably meant French – cuisines, this attitude was exaggerated in late nineteenth-century Australia, when the prevailing spirit was one of optimism and unbounded faith in a new country, seen through idealistic eyes as a land of promise. Such expression of dislike and distrust of foreign cuisine can be described as culinary xenophobia, and to the expatriates in Australia, foreign was synonymous with non-British. This attitude of culinary xenophobia paralysed the development of an Australian cuisine in what should have been its formative period, the second half of the nineteenth century.

Initial reports on Australia's gastronomic potential were downright unflattering, to say the least. In the 1830s, however, after the first

•

•

difficult decades had been survived, its natural resources were re-examined and its native inhabitants reappraised. Lieutenant Breton commended kangaroo meat at the same time as he recorded some of the Aboriginal dialectal names for various members of the marsupial family in New South Wales. James Atkinson, who in 1826 reported that there were no indigenous fruits worth eating, revised his opinion in 1844 to say that they had never received the attention they deserved. Robert Dawson, chief agent of the Australian Agricultural Company, enthused over the abundance of game and fish, and the vice-regal table gave indigenous produce the seal of approval. The ordinary citizens who congregated around the shores of Sydney Harbour turned oyster-gathering into a Sunday ritual.

Australia also offered a sympathetic home to plants and animals from other parts of the globe. 'I believe we can produce every European fruit and vegetable in perfection, and most, if not all, of the tropical vegetables and fruits', concluded Robert Dawson. Travellers were impressed by these natural benefits. Frank Fowler, a journalist who arrived in Australia in 1855 and edited several issues of the *Month* in 1858, described a 'typical' cottage on the edge of Sydney Harbour, with its banana palms and nectarine trees, citrus fruits and 'vines, all prodigal in purple clusters'. Charles Dilke, one of the most observant travellers to come to Australia in the nineteenth century, wrote about the Sydney market where 'not only are all the English fruits to be found, but plantains, guavas, loquats, pomegranates, pineapples from Brisbane, figs of every kind, and the delicious passionfruit'. In the words of J. Ewing Richie, Australia was a 'Paradise Regained'.

This enthusiasm was indicative of a new-found nationalism as immigration became a self-elected choice rather than an imposition.

In the words of the *Sydney Morning Herald* in 1849, Australia was now seen by immigrants as 'the land not only of their adoption [but] the land which by association, by the ties of family and connexions, had thoroughly become their own'. Just twenty years previously, the editorial continued, it had been merely 'a land to which we have no instinctive love, a country of adoption'.

With the gold rush of the 1850s came the beginnings of a distinctively Australian ethos. Population increased dramatically – an almost tenfold increase between 1851 and 1901 – but more importantly, it became more 'Australian'. By 1901, 82 per cent of the population had been born in the Australian colonies, when only fifty years previously the proportion was less than half. Australians, with their distinctive accent and manner of speech, were becoming recognisable, the language developing its own idioms, and Australians themselves were becoming aware of their own identity. They knew they were different from the immigrants fresh from England, the 'new chums' mocked for their ignorance of local ways. With the founding of the *Bulletin* in 1880, an Australian literary voice began to be heard, while artistic contemporaries initiated the 'Golden Summers' of Australian painting. The Comte de Beauvoir, visiting from France around this time, wrote: 'It seems that the Anglo-Saxon race has left on the other side of the equator everything which was blocking it in Europe, to resolutely take the path of progress here.'

In this climate, the foundations of an Australian cuisine could, and should, have been established. There was no shortage of ingredients, local or naturalised, nor of patriotic pride. And there were some who accepted the challenge. The first attempt at an Australian cuisine was made by Edward Abbott, in 1864, with his *English and Australian*

Cookery Book. This was something of a two-way bet, written both for the English housewife and 'her prototype in the Colonies'. Abbott enthusiastically commended the local Tasmanian game and fish and suggested appropriate ways of cooking them. In Queensland some twenty years later Mrs Lance Rawson (*The Antipodean Cookery Book*) and Mrs Maclurcan (*Mrs Maclurcan's Cookery Book: A Collection of Practical Recipes, Specially Suitable for Australia*) did likewise. Mrs Rawson also included several native fruits, giving recipes ('which I flatter myself are unknown to anyone else') for cooking and preserving them. Yet in all the books the ingredients, regardless of their origin, were cooked in a thoroughly English fashion, as if this were the only possible way, the 'British and Colonial mode', as Abbott described it. Moreover, it was a very basic English style, stripped of most of its regional and festive specialities by the lack of a cultural infrastructure. Cornish pasties survived in Australia because this old-country tradition of a portable lunch was retained by isolated groups of miners (who also helped the pasty to evolve, by adding pumpkin to the customary meat-potatoes-onions-turnips formula), but stargazy pie and saffron cake could not survive the shock of transplantation.

As if to add insult to injury, this basic English style of cooking – in Dr Philip Muskett's words, 'an endless recurrence of boiled potatoes, boiled cabbage, boiled this and that' and 'the conventional chain of joints, roasted or boiled, and the inevitable grill or fry' – was badly done. Cooking was regarded as women's work, and women were not necessarily skilled at, nor interested in, cooking. The incompetence of Australian cooks in the nineteenth century is well documented. In 1862 Godfrey Mundy wrote of the 'crowning disgrace of the colony! – wretched destitution in the earliest and worthiest of the sciences! –

there is no one – in a word, there is not a cook in New South Wales . . .
The cooks in this colony are no more cooks in the European and artis-
tical acceptation of the term, than any one of my coats would have
been a coat in the eyes of Brummel!' Philip Muskett agreed. 'The state
of affairs in the culinary art with the bulk of the people is simply
deplorable,' he wrote. Hardly surprising – cooks did not migrate in
great numbers to the Antipodes, and the class of women who needed
and employed cooks were often totally ignorant of any kitchen activity
and quite incapable of instructing and training novices.

Visiting Australia in 1888 for the International Centenary
Exhibition in Melbourne, the French journalist Oscar Comettant came
to a similar conclusion. 'There are two or three good restaurants in
Melbourne,' he noted.

> The rest are, to French palates, more or less bad. No more than in England
> do they know how to make stock in Australia . . . But, heavens above!
> What dreadful food you get in the cheap boarding houses and temperance
> hotels and restaurants! . . . The shilling meals consist of one of those
> soups that are neither soup nor sauce, a plate of tasteless meat
> accompanied by some even more tasteless vegetables boiled in saltless
> water, and a pudding that you swallow while reminding yourself that you
> must eat to live, not live to eat. That lot is washed down with plain water,
> more or less clear, or cooked water, more or less brown, called tea.

He fared much better in the private homes of the upper classes,
but restaurant food in general he found 'lacking in variety, and in the
true art of cooking. With this *cuisine* the appetite dies quickly.'

Cuisine, like language, travels with people, though in its new
environment it may be modified and evolve in a different direction

from that of the the homeland. White Australians were overwhelmingly of British stock, and it would be unreasonable to expect their style of cooking to have been anything but British – English, Irish, Scottish. As Philip Muskett remarked, 'The mode of living, and the mode of dress, which are followed in the old country, are slavishly copied in this part of the world.' Perhaps it is also unreasonable to expect that in a new country people would have taken more care in their cooking, paid more attention to the flavour of their food. But in addition to all this, the British brought with them their culinary xenophobia, the distrust of foreign food that was derided by Marcus Clarke.

It seems that Australia could welcome ingredients from all over the world, from cold-climate salmon to tropical fruits, but not foreign cuisines. Marcus Clarke might have glorified French cuisine but his opinions of Chinese food were far from flattering. Venturing into some of Melbourne's Chinese restaurants, he was disgusted by the 'horrible stenches that rolled out'. He described with obvious distaste the restaurant's offerings:

> Sucking-pig, roasted whole, was on the carte, and a curious mess, called by a name that sounded like 'foo-a-chow', and was compounded of sheep's trotters, sugar, cabbage, flour, and fish, smoked on the copper. The kitchen was appalling. Several boilers were simmering with all kinds of nastiness . . . We drank a teacup of 'sanshoo', a kind of vin ordinaire, with the sleek proprietor, and were thankful to depart.

Nor did Australians show much interest in learning from Aboriginal practices. Men may have had some experience of Aboriginal cuisine – that is, indigenous ingredients prepared and cooked by

Aboriginals in the Aboriginal manner – but such experiences were rare, and only exceptionally reached the domestic hearth.

So, at a time when signs of an Australian culture were beginning to appear in other arenas, the weight of British inheritance quashed the emergence of an Australian cuisine. Despite the prosperity of Australian society and the diversity of ingredients, the nation lacked the critical, adventurous and unprejudiced palates that would have encouraged successful attempts to break loose from the confines of custom. Thus was lost, for many years, the opportunity to harness nationalistic fervour to the bounty of the land.

A culinary tradition, like any other, takes many years to develop a reasonably stable core that can accept the fluctuations of fashion. Attempts to install an 'instant' cuisine by the aggressive appropriation of other cultures' recipes is foolhardy. The development of a culinary tradition requires a certain order and stability in society, and depends on the possibility of choice and the exercise of preference. With the right encouragement, it develops by means of inventions and modifications, of borrowings and adaptions from other cuisines, all of which were notably absent in the nineteenth century. Indigenous ingredients, and the harvest of land and sea, are fundamental to a cuisine but are not its raison d'être.

The opportunity to develop an Australian cuisine now exists. When we are least expecting it, we will turn around and find it there.

SCONES, SPONGES, ANZACS

AND LAMINGTONS

Sometimes chocolate or passionfruit icing topped the cake and the layers were filled with whipped cream that oozed from the sides as you squashed your wedge of cake down to mouth-size.

IN TURN-OF-THE-CENTURY Australian cities afternoon and morning teas, or 'at home' receptions, were a favoured means of entertaining among the social set, duly reported in the gossip columns of magazines such as *Table Talk*. These tea parties were often large affairs, frequently accompanied by music or some other sort of

•

•

entertainment. In the country, long after dinner parties and restaurant dining had replaced social teas as the done thing in the cities, the institution of afternoon tea lived on, especially on Sunday afternoons – leisure time on the farm.

In the search for a truly Australian cuisine, the kind practised in the typical domestic kitchen, the traditions of afternoon tea are often overlooked. And now that afternoon teas are fading from our consciousness, so too are the dishes that accompanied them. Coffee and cake is today's formula, and the cake is just as likely to be some crisp little Italian *biscotti*.

It's hardly surprising that this area of culinary endeavour has been neglected. Cakes and biscuits and afternoon tea fare are seen as frivolous accessories. They belong to the domain of women – women produced them, women consumed them. The afternoon teas at the Country Women's Association rooms provided women with solace and companionship on the occasional visits to town. Cakes and biscuits were not considered real food, men's food: a man needed meat to sustain him for fifteen miles of fencing after midday dinner.

Most people, when asked to describe a national cuisine or to cite typical examples, tend to overlook the domain of desserts and the sweet little nothings that don't make it to the main meal. Coq au vin would be more readily nominated as representative of French cuisine than crème caramel. Yet scones and sponges, anzacs and lamingtons are just as much part of Australian cuisine as crumbed cutlets and carpetbag steak. It's not that they rely on uniquely Australian ingredients, and whether or not they originated here is irrelevant (anzacs and lamingtons did, but not scones and sponges); what matters is that they have been cooked and eaten and enjoyed by generations of

Australians. They're as ordinary, familiar and important to our identity as backyards and barbecues. In addition, they're authenticated by that truly Australian institution, the country show.

Cooks who were obliged to defer to male appetites had little opportunity but to produce ample quantities of energy food, regularly, promptly and efficiently. Only on the one rest day of the week when constraints were temporarily removed, usually Sunday, could they escape from weekday monotony and indulge desires. It is clear from early recipe books that women's creativity went into the scones and cakes and biscuits that adorned the afternoon tea, rather than the soups and stews and roasts that represented the inevitable compromise with mutton, mutton, and yet more mutton. In Hal Porter's childhood home:

Saturday afternoon is for baking. This is a labour of double nature: to provide a week's supply of those more solid delicacies Australian mothers of those days regard as being as nutritionally necessary as meat twice daily, four vegetables at dinner, porridge and eggs and toast for breakfast, and constant cups of tea. Empty biscuit-barrels and cake-tins being as unthinkable as beds not made before eleven a.m., Mother, therefore, constructs a great fruit cake, and a score or more each of rock cakes, Banburies, queen cakes, date rolls and ginger nuts. These conventional solidities done, she exercises her talent for ritual fantasy, for the more costly and ephemeral dainties that are to adorn as fleetingly as day-lilies the altar of the Sunday tea-table. Now appear three-storeyed sponge cakes mortared together with scented cream and in whose seductive icing are embedded walnuts, silver cachous, glacé cherries, strawberries, segments of orange and strips of angelica. Now appear

cream puffs and éclairs, creations of the most momentary existence,
deliberately designed neither for hoarding against a rainy day nor for
social showing-off. Sunday tea is the frivolous and glittering crown of the
week; there is the impression given of throwing away money like delicious
dirt; there is the atmosphere rather than the fact of luxury; Sunday tea is,
above all, my parent's statement to each other and their children that
life is being lived on a plane of hard-earned and justifiable abundance.
I watch abundance which means that I watch Mother, its actual as well
as its symbolic impulse. – Hal Porter (1963)

Like most of the early colonists themselves, the dainties that were
served at afternoon tea came directly from England, Scotland and
Ireland. Balmoral tartlets, London buns, Banbury cakes, oat cakes and
rock cakes, cream puffs and brandy snaps, seed cake, spice cake and
Scotch shortbread, all these were part of the traditional British culinary
repertoire and travelled in the cultural baggage of the new settlers. It
was not difficult to reproduce them in the new country – eggs are eggs,
sugar is sugar, and butter is butter. These tea-time staples were per-
petuated in early Australian recipe books, such as *The Cookery Book of*
Good and Tried Receipts and *The Practical Australian Cookery*, both
published at the end of the nineteenth century. Like many of their
contemporaries, these books offered simple, practical, economical
recipes, thoroughly English in style but often with a discernible
Australian character. Most of the biscuits and cakes that fill their pages
were not born in Australia but became Australian by adoption and,
little by little, developed Australian characteristics of their own, such as
passionfruit filling and icing for a plain butter cake.

One particular kind of cake became more Australian than the

●

●

rest: the high and handsome sponge. Even higher on its cut-glass pedestal, it was the supreme symbol of the afternoon tea table. Now, the sponge has quite a long pedigree. In 1747 Hannah Glasse gave a recipe for little sponge 'biskits' made simply with eggs, sugar and flour. More than a century later Edward Abbott included a sponge recipe in the very first Australian cookery book, *The English and Australian Cookery Book* (1864). He prescribed a pound of flour, a pound of sugar and eight eggs, separated: the same ingredients as Mrs Glasse, in the same proportions.

Like rabbits, the sponge flourished in Australia and soon there was a whole family of sponges: the blowaway sponge, a very light cake that used a small volume of flour, mostly arrowroot; the neverfail sponge, with eggs and sugar beaten for an exceptionally long time; the cornflour sponge, similar to blowaway but using cornflour instead of arrowroot; and many other variations. Sponge-making was elevated to an art form. Hints abounded: use duck eggs, said some; day-old eggs, said others, and make sure you sift the flour three times. Good recipes were prized but it was less the recipe than the hands that made it that ensured success.

Jam, with or without whipped cream, was the standard filling for a sponge sandwich, its top often speckled with a cloud of powdered icing sugar. Sifted over a paper doily, the sugar produced a snowy pattern of leaves, arabesques, and curlicues. Sometimes chocolate or passionfruit icing topped the cake and the layers were filled with whipped cream that oozed from the sides as you squashed your wedge of cake down to mouth-size. As the sponge family multiplied, the flavour went into the cake itself: chocolate, coffee, cinnamon, ginger, and lemon were all popular. Sometimes the cake was baked in a long sheet, spread with raspberry jam, and rolled into a sponge roll. (These I remember with greatest pleasure, partly because they were cream-less and less cumbersome to eat, but mostly for the sweet crunchiness of the sugar-encrusted edge.)

Other staples of the tea table – and of the children's lunch box – were also British in origin, Australian by adoption: the multi-layered rainbow cake, chocolate-iced marble cake, date and nut loaves, gin-gerbread, gem scones and pikelets. Some, originally of British stock, were born and raised here, such as the Australian brownie, an eco-nomical, foolproof, long-lasting fruit loaf that is a regular at shearers' smokos; and the Australian variant of boiled fruitcake, made with a can of crushed pineapple. Others again may be of mixed parentage – such as butterfly cakes, small cup cakes with a circular wedge cut from the top, the hollow filled with whipped cream, and the two halves of the wedge placed on the cream so as to look like butterfly wings. They are now as completely and unmistakably Australian as merinos and kelpies – and perhaps just as clichéd.

Supper. The coffee-urn and trestle table laden with sausage rolls, anzacs, rainbow cake, date-loaf, and pavlova were waiting at the end of the hall, presided over by two large-bosomed ladies who had spent the whole of my talk in setting it up, its impressive abundance determined less by the size of the audience than by their own sense of what was due to the Arts – the Arts, out here, meaning Cookery, of which the higher forms are cake decoration and the ornamental bottling of carrots. – David Malouf (1985)

But the three best-known relics of our culinary creativity are the all-Australian originals of lamingtons, anzac biscuits and pumpkin scones. Lamingtons – apparently named after Lord Lamington,

•

•

governor of Queensland from 1895 to 1901 – made their debut around the turn of the century. Popular myth supposes these cake cubes, dipped in thin chocolate icing and rolled in coconut, to have been invented as a resourceful way of using up stale sponge cake (instead of turning it into trifle!), but this seems doubtful, given that in 1902 one of the earliest recipes instructs the cook to begin by making a plain butter sponge. Today they might be considered lumpish and unlovely but, like sausage sizzles, lamington drives in aid of schools and clubs and local charities are part of Australian popular culture. At Stephanie's restaurant in Melbourne, Stephanie Alexander sometimes serves a lamington dessert: a lamington cake accompanied by a trompe-l'oeil lamington of coconut icecream, coated in chocolate and rolled in coconut, together with a small square of coconut ice.

Anzac biscuits were probably baptised during the first world war when they were apparently sent to soldiers as a gift from home, though they didn't make the recipe books until the 1920s. They, too, have non-indigenous coconut (always spelled cocoanut in the early recipe books) as a major ingredient, and could have developed as a variation on the coconut-less soldier biscuits. Pumpkin scones date from about the same era, though since they probably owe their genesis to a surfeit of pumpkin they might have been appearing on tea tables long before they made it to the printed page. They seem to have been invented in Queensland, the state that gave us Queensland blue, the paragon of pumpkins.

So with at least three born-and-bred-in-Australia recipes, and many other dainties adopted and naturalised, the afternoon tea repertoire justifiably claims recognition in the definitive book of Australian cuisine. They represent the ritual of a disappearing era – lazy afternoons, cane chairs on the verandah, compliments on the sponge, and dust storms on the horizon – but are no less characteristically Australian for all that.

Industrialisation means that sponges now come from the freezer or the packet ('just add water') and the Magimix-microwave revolution has introduced a completely new style of cake. It is the nature of cuisine to evolve with changes in society. Carême's patisserie master-pieces are no longer constructed (if they ever were) to grace the tables of diplomatic dinners, yet they are still considered to belong within French cuisine. The sponges, scones and butterfly cakes that adorned the afternoon tea tables of past generations are as much a part of Australian cuisine as the hundreds-and-thousands fairy bread of children's parties. Like the crumbed cutlet and carpetbag steak, they deserve an honourable place in our gastronomic hall of fame.

THE RISE AND DEMISE

OF THE KANGAROO STEAMER

Kangaroos come originally from Australia and the surrounding islands. Essentially fruit eaters in their wild state, kangaroos are very easy to feed when tame. They decide to eat everything which is offered to them and, it is said, even drink wine and brandy when these are given to them. – Alexandre Dumas

ON 12 JULY 1862, the Acclimatisation Society of Great Britain held a special 'Australian' dinner, the menu for which included such novelties as kangaroo steamer (entree), kangaroo ham and rosella jelly.

•

•

According to Edward Abbott, author of *The English and Australian Cookery Book* (1864), Sir John Maxwell 'pronounced it [the kangaroo steamer] excellent, as a stew, and said he would like to see it introduced into the Navy'. Flushed with patriotic pride, of course Abbott would give the steamer a good press. He even said that Napoleon wanted to introduce the kangaroo into France, so good was its meat.

The kangaroo steamer: obsolete, say the dictionaries, bluntly. History treats it more sympathetically, showing us that the kangaroo steamer enjoyed its century or so of glory, rapturously praised by those who tasted it. 'But of all the dishes ever brought to table, nothing equals that of the steamer', wrote Henry Melville in 1851. Melville described how the dish was made 'by mincing the flesh of the kangaroo, and with it some pieces of pork or bacon. The animal has not any fat, or scarcely any, in its best season. When the meat is chopped up, it is thrown into a saucepan, and covered with the lid, and left to stew or steam gently by the fireside. It is, from this method of cooking, called a "steamer". People generally put a spoonful of water in the pot when they place it on the fire; but this is unnecessary, as the flesh soon floats in its own rich gravy. It only requires pepper and salt to render it delicious'.

The first written reference to the kangaroo steamer was in Tasmania – then still Van Diemen's Land – in 1820. Even at this early stage, it seems to have been a fairly common dish in both that colony and New South Wales. Significantly, the *Oxford English Dictionary* records 'steamer', as a dish, as of Australian origin. But if it was unique to Australia, our first contribution to the world's cuisine, where did it come from, why did it fade ignominiously away, and what did it say during its lifetime?

•

•

In the pioneering years of the colonies kangaroo was sometimes the principal source of fresh meat. In Sydney in 1796 kangaroo meat sold for sixpence a pound, compared with a shilling per pound for salt pork and two shillings for mutton. During the first years of settlement in Van Diemen's Land convicts were issued a ration of 8 lb. of kangaroo meat per week, and in six months the settlers (including convicts) ate 15,000 lb. of kangaroo haunches and tails. Even in the 1840s, kangaroo meat was sold in Hobart when supplies of other fresh meats were scarce. Explorers and adventurers hunted, killed, cooked and ate kangaroo rather than carry supplies of preserved foods. For those colonists fully occupied in clearing land, erecting shelters and building up livestock herds, kangaroos were like a magic pudding, dinner hopping around on two legs. While they sampled other game – quail, emu, bandicoots, possums – kangaroo was the preferred quarry. In a letter to Eliza Acton, written from the Bendigo gold fields in 1853, William Howitt quipped: 'But it is at this end of the world as at the other "first catch your hare" – no – it is a little different – "first catch your Kangaroo, and then cook it".'

Kangaroos not only represented food but provided sport. 'Coursing the kangaroo and emu forms the principal amusement of the sporting part of the colonists,' wrote William Wentworth in 1820. 'Kangarooing' was apparently so common by the 1860s that a humorous poem was written about it and became a bush ballad, 'Going kangarooing', sung to the tune of 'King of the Cannibal Isles'. The kangaroo hunt developed its own etiquette, part of which involved the presentation of the kangaroo tail to a favoured lady in imitation of the English custom whereby the lady was given the 'brush' of the fox. In Australia this tail was turned into kangaroo tail soup.

The kangaroo was chosen as the object of the transplanted ritualised hunt partly because of the exhilaration of the chase. In addition, kangaroos were plentiful, they offered a large target and were easy to skin. Possums are nocturnal, quail fiddly to pluck and prepare; wombats live underground and, in Tasmania at least, emus were quickly hunted to extinction. But perhaps a more persuasive reason for expatriate English to choose the kangaroo is that its meat had a close resemblance to familiar meats and was more tasty, more palatable than that of other indigenous animals, often being compared to hare or venison. Certainly, early recipe books tend to have more recipes for kangaroo than other game. Abbott includes seven recipes for kangaroo, one each for emu, wombat and mutton bird. Author Louisa Meredith ate barbecued kangaroo in Tasmania in the early 1850s and reported that 'kangaroo is, in fact, very like hare.'

That kangaroo was likened to hare offers a clue to the origins of the steamer. It could hardly have been derived from a cooking practice of the Aboriginal inhabitants, who cooked without pots (and who, in Tasmania at least, seem to have been hunted almost as much as was the kangaroo). Traditional English game cookery of the eighteenth and early nineteenth centuries makes no mention of a 'steamer', but it does introduce the technique of 'jugging', cooking in a closed earthenware 'jug'. 'Jugged hare' apparently dates from about the mid-eighteenth century: the OED records its first usage in 1747 in *The Art of Cookery*, by Hannah Glasse. Mrs Glasse's recipe calls for the hare to be cut in little pieces, larded with 'little Slips of Bacon', seasoned with pepper and salt and laid in an earthenware jug with a blade or two of mace, an onion stuck with cloves and a bundle of sweet herbs. 'Cover the Jugg or Jar you do it in, so close, that nothing can get in, then set it in a Pot of boiling Water' and let it cook for three hours.' The ingredients and the technique are surprisingly similar. From English jugged hare to Australian kangaroo steamer is but one short step.

Whether or not they called it 'jugging', Englishmen (and women) who came to Australia in the early years of the nineteenth century are likely to have been familiar with the simple technique described by Hannah Glasse. It was easily adapted to open-fire and hearth-side cooking, and the new colonists applied it to the ingredients around them: kangaroo meat, which was plentiful; and bacon, which was imported into the colonies from the earliest days. The standard seasonings and flavourings would also have been readily available. And they called it a steamer – because, as they observed and recorded, the dish steamed. Kangaroo steamer, then, was the antipodean equivalent of jugged hare.

But while jugged hare, in England, developed into a more complex dish with thickened gravy and forcemeat balls, kangaroo steamer was at the end of its evolutionary branch and gradually became extinct. By the end of the century, references to the steamer were becoming scarce. There are no kangaroo recipes in *The Australian Cook* (1876), by Alfred Wilkinson, though this Chef de Cuisine of the Athenaeum Club in Melbourne did use local game such as rabbit, hare and wild duck, and his recipe for jugged rabbit or hare reads very much like a steamer. Nor are there any kangaroo recipes in *Mrs Maclurcan's Cookery Book* (1898), though it offers a recipe for jugged wallaby. The steamer's age of glory was fast approaching an end. Born in the fledgling colonies and bush, it had no place in the rapidly growing cities where among the elite at the turn of the century, French cuisine had come to represent the epitome of civilised living.

•

•

Nevertheless, *The Goulburn Cookery Book* by Mrs Rutledge (first published 1899) features a recipe for Steamed Kangaroo or Wallaby that differs little from Abbott's recipe of 1864:

STEAMED KANGAROO OR WALLABY

Kangaroo or wallaby, salt pork or bacon, 2 or 3 onions, 1/2 wineglass of ketchup, 1 claret glass of port wine, pepper, salt.

Cut the kangaroo into pieces about the size of a small veal cutlet, and slice the pork or bacon. Put a layer of pork at the bottom of a gourmet boiler or earthenware jar, then a layer of kangaroo, then onions. Season with salt and plenty of pepper. Continue these layers until all is used. Cover with a cloth, and then put on the lid; see that it fits well, so that no steam escapes. Put the pot in a saucepan half full of boiling water, and cook for 4 hours. Half an hour before serving, add the ketchup, and 20 minutes afterwards a claret glass of port. Serve with a dish of hot boiled rice.

Mrs Rutledge wrote her book for 'women in the bush'. By the turn of the century, these women in the bush were very much a minority, since about two-thirds of the Australian population lived in the capital cities and larger country towns. The majority of the population would hardly have had the opportunity to try kangaroo, even had they wished to do so. There is no evidence that kangaroo was available in the towns, and if it had been, any sales would probably have been under-the-counter. Since most recipe books published in the early years of the twentieth century were directed to this highly urbanised population, the kangaroo steamer gradually faded from print as it disappeared from tables. The last report comes from

The CWA Cookery Book and Household Hints, a collection of recipes from Country Women's Association ladies, first published in Perth in 1936. The book's recipe for Kangaroo Steamer came from the Bunbury Branch, and calls for one pound of kangaroo steak minced with half a pound of bacon, then mixed with one cup of breadcrumbs and one teaspoon of mixed herbs, tied up in a cloth and boiled 'quietly' for three hours. The basic ingredients (kangaroo and bacon) are right, but its preparation is virtually the same as for Aberdeen Sausage, one of the standard recipes in cookbooks of the early twentieth century. Abbott and his colonial mates would never recognise it as a succulent 'steamer'.

There are many possible explanations for the demise of the kangaroo steamer from the late nineteenth century. First is the extraordinarily high concentration of Australians in cities and towns; people no longer lived off the land, and kangaroo meat was hardly an item of commerce. As the pastoral industries flourished, the more prestigious beef and mutton became cheaper and more easily accessible. According to Jock Marshall and Russell Drysdale, 'as recently as a little before the turn of the century, kangaroo chops and 'roo-tail soup figured on the menus of city hotels. With increased production of cheap mutton and beef, bush foods disappeared from "good" tables.' Another explanation is the fashion for 'dainty dishes' which began around the turn of the century, gradually spread by such magazines as the *Australian Home Journal*.

Even in rural Australia, it's likely that the prime ingredient, kangaroo, was less plentiful. As early as 1820 Jeffreys warned of the risk of extinction if 'wholesale and indiscriminate destruction' were not prevented. Some thirty years later Louisa Meredith reported that the

Forester kangaroo had been so hunted that very few were left in Tasmania. While there were still many in the grazing areas of western Victoria, she believed that these, too, would soon be recklessly destroyed by pastoralists who wanted to remove all threat of competition to their livestock. There's no doubt pastoralists saw kangaroos as competition. The Melbourne *Argus* of 1860 reported that, since 100 kangaroos eat as much as 200 sheep, 'the destruction of these obnoxious marauders must therefore have in it some utility and merit'. Kangaroos stood in the way of profit. No longer were they seen as an alternative source of food, but rather as competition to the production of 'real' food (mutton) and income.

Here is the clue to the disappearance of the steamer: people no longer valued kangaroo, no longer appreciated the meat. If they went on a hunt it was purely for the sport. History shows that a dish, born out of a certain spirit of place and time, passes away when the environment (cultural and physical) and values that supported it are no longer present. The kangaroo steamer belongs to Australia's formative period, when adventurous settlers were making a new life in a new land, and their innocent enthusiasm is evident in their delight in living off the land. No doubt this was a necessity in some circumstances, but it was also a way of appropriating the land and affirming a relationship with it, an expression of identity. These new settlers were proudly Australian. Taller, leaner, tanned and weatherbeaten, their appearance distinguished them from their kinsmen who remained 'at home'. In character, too, they were recognisably different, and as G.C. Mundy observed, these differences were proclaimed through what they ate. He describes a dinner in Sydney in 1851:

————— ⅏ —————

The family likeness between an Australian and an Old Country dinner-party became, however, less striking when I found myself sipping doubtfully, but soon swallowing with relish, a plate of wallabi-tail soup, followed by a slice of boiled schnapper, with oyster sauce. A haunch of kangaroo venison helped to convince me that I was not in Belgravia. A delicate wing of the wonga-wonga pigeon and bread sauce, with a dessert of plantains and loquots, guavas and mandarine oranges, pomegranates and cherimoyas, landed my imagination at length fairly at the Antipodes.

At the start of the twentieth century, when Australia was one of the most urbanised countries of the world, when the basis of a national identity had been laid and the initial brashness and rawness tempered, when railway systems could ensure prompt delivery of city goods to isolated country sidings, when open hearths had been replaced by gas ranges, the kangaroo steamer was an anomaly. Too closely associated with the privations of bush-pioneering days, it represented another opportunity lost. Its creation had symbolised the potential of this new environment; it had facilitated the transition from an old culture to a developing one. Having served its purpose, the steamer could now be decently retired.

Not only kangaroo steamer but also kangaroo virtually disappeared from Australian tables. Not that it was illegal to sell kangaroo meat, as long as it was prepared under conditions that allowed it to be passed as fit for human consumption, but there was simply no demand.

Nor was there any demand this century until the 1980s, when the coincidence of two powerful sentiments put kangaroo on the menu again. First was an increasing concern for the environment, and the

•

•

recognition of the damage done to fragile natural environments by hard-hoofed animals such as sheep and cattle. Second was a resurgence of interest in Australian cuisine and renewed awareness of national identity. In the late 1970s, a South Australian company, Jesser Meats, established separate premises for the treatment of kangaroo so that it did not come into contact with other products destined for pet food and began to market kangaroo meat. It also offered some to Malaysian-born chef Cheong Liew, who was the first to experiment with it at his Adelaide restaurant, Neddy's, initially preparing it as thin medallions, Chinese-style. The reintroduction of kangaroo meat, and its acceptance on Australian tables, is due to Cheong's perseverance and to the enthusiasm of another chef/restaurateur, Maggie Beer, who began to feature it on the game-slanted menu of her Barossa Valley restaurant.

These developments happened at a time when nouvelle cuisine facilitated – indeed, almost obliged – experimentation and innovation in the kitchen. Restaurants which had called themselves 'French' – and 'French' had been the accepted model for fine cuisine – began to call themselves 'Creative' or 'Eclectic'. By 1995 the numbers of 'French' restaurants listed in guide books had been decimated, and 'Modern Australian' formed by far the largest single restaurant category. Kangaroo, unreservedly Australian, is one of the hallmarks of 'Mod Oz', and happily lends itself to a multiplicity of treatments and garnishes to yield dishes that are a long way from the minimalist simplicity of the kangaroo steamer. Grilled fillet of kangaroo with red wine glaze and smoked kangaroo with onion and chilli jam aptly illustrate Australian gastronomic identity at the end of the twentieth century, as kangaroo steamer proudly symbolised the spirit of early Australia.

•

•

REGIONALISM IN AUSTRALIA

The kitchen is a country in which there are always discoveries to be made. — Grimod de La Reynière

--- ---

IF THE 1980S WAS the era of nouvelle cuisine, the 1990s is set to be the decade of regionalism. Raymond Sokolov, who in the 1970s recorded the 'fading feasts' of America, wryly observed a decade later that: 'People I had interviewed in the ultimate boondocks of the country in order to record the death of the regionalism they were still preserving turned up in food-page articles as purveyors of luxury specialities to Manhattan and Los Angeles restaurants.'

One might cynically observe that near-saturation of the cook-

•

•

book market demands increasing specialisation. Or, more charitably, take a broader view and point to a worldwide movement in the second half of the twentieth century for some degree of regional autonomy, from the Basques to the Bretons (linguistically), culminating in the disintegration of uneasy unions in eastern Europe. But in the world of food, the vogue for regionalism seems to me to be also a reaction to the internationalism of nouvelle cuisine, at the same time as being its direct extension.

Regionalism goes hand-in-hand with tourism which, at the end of the twentieth century, has come to mean big money. Countries, states, regions, all want to attract tourists and their credit cards, and in a competitive arena each must be able to show that it has something special that other countries, states, regions do not have – beaches or mountains, historic houses or fabulous shopping, exotic gardens or national parks. And something deliciously different by way of food and drink, since all tourists want to eat and, if possible, enhance their travel experiences through food, sampling barramundi and buffalo in Darwin, camel and kangaroo in Alice Springs. Thus the search for regional specialities and regional cuisines. Tourism, which at the beginning of this century happened upon and 'discovered' the hidden regional cuisines of France, is today, ironically, the driving force behind their development in Australia.

Regional food and drink specialities are generally easier to identify and promote than regional cuisines. In France several different systems have been set up for this express purpose, one of which is the IGP – *Indication Géographique Protégée* – a kind of appellation effectively equivalent to that applied to wine. The fishing port of Collioure on the western Mediterranean coast, for example, has applied for recognition of its anchovies under this system. It's a guarantee of quality but also a vehicle for promoting the anchovies, thus ensuring the continuation of local industry and tradition. Similarly, Castelnaudary has applied for IGP recognition of the appellation '*cassoulet de Castelnaudary*'. For years a large sign outside the town has proclaimed Castelnaudary 'world capital of *cassoulet*', a hearty dish of white beans, fresh pork, pork sausage and duck *confit* cooked in an earthenware *cassole*. Local producers and vendors of *cassoulet* are now seeking its official authentication, fearful of seeing a deeply rooted local tradition become dispersed and deformed through the proliferation of supermarket cuisine.

Certainly, the IGP certification can give selected products a competitive edge in the marketplace, but at the same time it ensures quality, encourages the continuance of local skills and traditions and promotes a sense of regional identity. These are also the motivating forces behind the series of guides sponsored by the National Council of Culinary Arts in France, collectively known as the Inventory of the Culinary Heritage of France (*L'inventaire du patrimoine culinaire de la France*). Each book contains a catalogue of regional products (foods and beverages, both raw ingredients and manufactured products) that meet the pre-defined criteria, a selection of regional recipes, both traditional and 're-invented' by celebrated chefs of that region, together with a comprehensive bibliography and a contact list of names of producer organisations and associated professional groups. In calling attention to the gastronomic riches of the regions these books are as much for locals as for tourists.

Seals of authenticity are destined to become more and more prevalent throughout Europe as local and regional specialities are

●

●

detailed, catalogued and systematised. The French, who are probably the most vigorous in such activities, have a long history of classifying and certifying, beginning with the classification of Bordeaux wines in 1855. The gastronomic guides to the various regions of France have inspired the extension of the cataloguing scheme to cover the whole of Europe, under the banner of the Euroterroirs Project. It will eventually produce a database of about 4,000 European regional food specialities such as the Denby Dale Pie, an enormous celebratory beef-and-potato pie baked approximately every 25 years in the village of Denby Dale, West Yorkshire, England. The information collected will be published as a comprehensive encyclopaedia, together with smaller volumes for each country. The project does not merely represent information for information's sake; it may also generate naming schemes (appellations) and promote tourism and rural development. The IGP certification seems to go further in that it's not simply an assurance of quality but also a kind of rallying banner for regional patriots.

Australia has not (yet) produced inventories or catalogues or certifying schemes for foods, but there is increasing recognition of regional specialities – Young cherries and Bowen mangoes, King Island beef and Kangaroo Island sheep milk cheeses, Queensland mud crabs and South Australian King George whiting, Tasmanian leatherwood honey and Riverland dried fruit. Oysters are increasingly identified as to their place of origin and Mudgee wines have their own appellation. And now that 'Australian' cuisine has achieved some kind of status, the quest for distinctive regional characters has engaged attention. But is it now, and will it ever be, possible to speak of regional cuisines in Australia? Or will we have to be content with showcasing the bounty of a particular area and inviting ingenious chefs to create one-off dishes from these ingredients, as if to demonstrate a potential regionality? Can regional cuisines be invented by compiling an inventory of local resources and announcing a recipe competition? Should a regional cuisine reflect the practices and preferences of the inhabitants, so that it develops from the ground up, as it were – or can it be imposed by 'experts'?

Years ago, when people in Australia were far more reliant on local produce, you could find regional specialities based on ingredients proper to the region. Most of them are probably now extinct. In Australia today, when the typical dinner is laconically described as 'meat-and-veg', what people eat anywhere in the continent more frequently reflects what is available on supermarket shelves – which might mean cheese from another state, fish fingers from New Zealand and canned fruit from anywhere in the world. At the same time, para-doxically, the different regions are producing an exciting diversity of quality foods – specialised cheeses and smallgoods, farmed freshwater crustaceans, unusual varieties of fruits and vegetables.

Ingredients alone cannot make a cuisine, nor does a cuisine spring spontaneously from the ingredients. Whatever authentic food traditions exist in Australia may have had their roots in particular ingredients, whether indigenous or naturalised, but from the kangaroo steamer to the quandong pie to the pumpkin scone they also needed the mediation of culture. None of these specialities was particularly 'regional' – in the early days, the kangaroo steamer was eaten in both the colonies of New South Wales and Van Diemen's Land. Quandong pie probably originated in the period of pastoral expansion and was presumably made wherever and whenever quandongs were found.

Pumpkin scones were born of a surplus of pumpkins, often the only vegetable that could be grown in the outback. But these are isolated examples, and can hardly be said to constitute a cuisine.

A regional cuisine is usually epitomised by a collection of recognised dishes that depend on certain locally available ingredients and illustrate certain flavour combinations and cooking and preparation methods characteristic of, if not particular to, the region. These dishes might appear daily, or seasonally, or for particular festivities. Often they rely on local produce, but this is not a necessary pre-condition – think of all the regional specialities around the Mediterranean based on imported salt cod. Often they belong to the repertoire of the domestic cook, but they might also be restaurant specialities or products of the butcher or pastrycook. They are recognised and claimed by the people of the region.

In Australia there have been attempts to coax some semblance of regional cuisine into existence through imaginative combinations of local ingredients. About ten years ago a recipe competition to promote the use of local (regional) ingredients in the McLaren Vale wine area in South Australia was won by a recipe for 'Cinnamon-and-tea-smoked duck breast with pickled black olives, almonds and blackberry glaze'. Admittedly, the purpose of this contest was not to encourage the development of a regional cuisine, nor to enhance awareness of this possibility. It was simply a recipe competition – like the ones that used to be run by flour or margarine manufacturers – in quest of a dish displaying originality in the use of local ingredients. Yet the winning recipe was presented for tasting at the local Bushing Festival some months later, almost as if it were, or could be, an example of the local cuisine. Its fate was to be forgotten.

In Aragon the *Lanzon* was immediately accepted as part of the region's cuisine because it represented the people's desire to express themselves as Aragonese. Similarly, experience in Canada has shown that trying to artificially create or resuscitate regional cuisines succeeds best when there's already some awareness of regional identity, some cultural cohesion.

In an endeavour to promote regional cuisines in Quebec, a state with almost twice as much colonial history behind it as Australia, the province was divided into a number of geographic divisions, and in each one church groups and other community organisations were asked to collect their favourite recipes as the basis for an inventory of local ingredients and local dishes. After much grading, correlating and organising, a selection of more than 30,000 recipes was assembled to be tested in the kitchens of the Institut de Tourisme et d'Hotellerie du Québec. The best of these were referred back to local regional committees for their deliberation. Those approved were returned to the Institut for re-testing, and for standard quantities to be established.

Eventually, a book was published: *Cuisine du Québec*, a collection of 600-odd recipes said to typify the regional cuisines of the province. However, because the 'regions' were constructed more-or-less according to administrative divisions and did not necessarily correspond to any cultural reality, many Quebec residents believe the whole bureaucratic exercise to have been futile. The only real regional cuisines, they contend, are to be found around Quebec city, which has remained more stolidly French, and in multicultural Montreal, which welcomed a stream of immigrants over a century ago. Further, they point out that the most commonly eaten dish throughout the whole province is of Italo-American derivation, spaghetti with a meat-

and-tomato sauce. (What they could also point out is that it is a typically *Québecois* meat-and-tomato sauce, seasoned with the spices that characterise much of the cooking of Quebec and, incidentally, the same ones that were common in France several hundred years ago: cloves, cinnamon and allspice.)

Australian regions are not well defined, culturally, but if there's a case for the promotion of regional cuisines in Australia, the Barossa Valley must be one of the first to be nominated. Of all the potential 'regions' of Australia, it has perhaps the greatest claim to individuality. Gastronomically it is largely self-sufficient. Alongside the vast vineyards of the large wine companies are the mixed holdings of small farmers. In the towns butchers and bakers continue to practise the old crafts of smoking, sausage-making and yeast cookery. The Barossa has a biennial vintage festival, an annual Gourmet Weekend, and an annual music festival. There's a sense of regional identity in the closely linked triangle of towns and, since a significant proportion of the population is directly or indirectly dependent on the wine industry, a degree of cultural and economic unity.

Further, the Barossa has a long-standing reputation for fine food, a quality often associated with a recognised regional cuisine. Mention to a Frenchman that you're going to, say, Burgundy, and he'll smack his lips, rub his hands together and assure you, with patriotic emotion, '*Ah, oui, on mange bien en Bourgogne.*' My second edition of *The Barossa Cookery Book* (first published 1917, and surely one of the first regional cookery books in Australia) is subtitled: *Four Hundred Selected Recipes* FROM A DISTRICT CELEBRATED THROUGHOUT AUSTRALIA FOR THE EXCELLENCE OF ITS COOKERY (my emphasis!).

All this would seem to favour the existence of a Barossa regional cuisine. Certainly, the Barossa does have some genuinely traditional dishes, whether of German or Anglo-Saxon origin or a hybrid of the two. Local traditions – such as dill pickles – still exist in the home kitchen, along with the handed-down hand-written recipe books in a spidery script. Family customs have been retained in some households, even if their German origins have by now been forgotten. Some of the traditions belong to religious festivals, others are associated with everyday eating: dumplings, noodle soups, cream-and-vinegar dressing for salads of shredded lettuce (or sliced cucumber, or tomato and onion) – a dressing that, incidentally, is an echo of the tradition of the Alsace region of north-eastern France, climatically and geographically not too far distant from the homeland of the first immigrant Silesian farm workers.

But in Australia the repository for the cuisine of a region is usually assumed to be its restaurants, where the homely products of the domestic family kitchen rarely appear. So what is represented as Barossa cuisine is more likely to be the deliberate creation of the restaurant kitchen, the product of gastronomic rationalism. It uses local produce and ingredients, certainly, but seems designed more to harmonise with the region's Mediterranean climate than to reflect the cultural heritage of a large proportion of its population. While there is a certain logic to a resource-based regionality, it should also be recognised as an artifice. Cuisine, after all, is the product of ingredients and people, and however unfashionable or politically incorrect popular practices might be, they should not be ignored.

Regionalism in Australia is not as deeply rooted, nor as well cultivated, as in Tuscany, for example, or in Normandy in France, but it could be encouraged and nurtured. Beginning with an awareness of the region's identity, its unique character – gastronomic, historic, ethnic – a regional cuisine can start to develop. It requires local ingredients, whether or not these are particular to the region, and it should respect the seasons as well as local customs and practices. It should be featured in the region's restaurants but be equally adaptable to domestic kitchens so that it can be proudly presented in the home. But most of all, perhaps, it needs patience and the realisation that a cuisine cannot be created overnight. If the cuisine is truly to represent the region it has to last longer than fashion.

AN AUSTRALIAN BANQUET,

1984

For there is an aspect of cruelty in eating, nourishing one life at the expense of another.

THE SETTING: CARCLEW, a stately old Adelaide mansion, its massive, crude-cut stone facade illuminated by diffuse beams of light from sources below the lawns. Rosemary bushes guard the entrance and a gravel path leads to the front door, beyond which is the foyer and the long, high-ceilinged former ballroom, scene of the evening's banquet.

•

•

The players: forty-eight people from all over Australia (and one from England) who have attended the First Symposium of Australian Gastronomy, and who have, for two whole days, discussed, practised, argued and contemplated gastronomy: its past and present, its future in Australia.

It is deep night as we arrive; the blackness is pierced here and there by the brilliant white of floodlights. The house is sealed and curtained. No noise escapes, there is no whisper of behind-the-scenes activity. Suddenly out of the darkness appears a white-faced Pierrot, leaping Nijinsky-like through the garden. He bows low, gestures to us to approach the main door, and dissolves again into the darkness.

The foyer is bright, animated, already crowded. Softly, intermittently, music wafts down from a quintet of Pierrots on the landing and evaporates into the atmosphere. More black-and-white-costumed Pierrots offer aperitifs of pale dry sherry or ruby-pink sparkling burgundy, more popular and more appropriate to the mood of the guests, as excited as children before a birthday party. The dinner is late, and this unprogrammed delay intensifies the anticipation and suspense. Then, unexpectedly, another Pierrot bounds on to the stairs, and the music and crowd hush as he announces: 'Cooks, food philosophers, nutritionists, passionate amateurs, dinner is served!'

Single file, we quietly enter the transformed room, now practically devoid of decor – blank walls, dim and muted lighting. Within the frame of the room, and in the form of a long rectangle with one open side, are white-covered tables, interrupted at predetermined intervals by squares of black, the whole lavishly strewn with rose petals and roses of many colours. Nothing else on the tables, save the white napkin squares at each place – no intimation that a banquet is to take place. But from the doorway, our eyes light on the first item of the menu, displayed on one of the black squares: Jellied Seascape.

It is so realistic that no one can be quite sure that it is meant to be eaten. We gaze at this large glass aquarium, murkily translucent, where seaweeds and sea creatures co-exist. On one wall a delicately delineated sea plant seems to move to its own mysterious rhythm, on another we notice the sinister suckers of an octopus groping toward the surface flotsam. We admire it all, in a detached and objective way, but our palates are wary of savouring nature undisguised.

Seated, we whisper with our neighbours, marvelling at the originality of the seascape, theorising on the practical aspects of its creation, wondering what act will follow. From the ballroom alcove the musicians continue, their shrill flute-like sounds evocative of medieval instruments. We watch entranced as a sequence of mute Pierrots lay knives and forks, arrange glasses, pour wine: and we begin to realise that this evening we are captive, dependent on these pantomime characters for all our needs.

Along and across tables conversations continue until, abruptly, order is imposed by the soft beat of drums announcing the arrival of the dishes of the first service. Five of them – the Jellied Seascape is already in place – are paraded up and down between the two rows of diners, winning spontaneous applause and exciting appetites. The platters are set down on the black squares and some of us, unable to restrain our curiosity, leave our places to take a closer view – of the steaming silver cauldron of consommé, in which float tiny wonton; of the large silver salver bearing individual molds of lambs' brains, each enrobed in transparently thin slivers of zucchini and flanked by delicate slices of tongue. And there's another huge tray, unadorned save for the solid, glistening block of truffle-coated Goose Liverwurst, across which is nonchalantly arranged a pale and fleshy sausage of the same mixture.

We are offered servings from the dish nearest to hand, and for a while are oblivious to any sensation but that of the food on our palates. Delicious, seductively delicious: the meltingly soft textures of the brains and tongues, the gingery sweetness of their sauce, the rich decadence of the liverwurst. After a temporary disappearance, the Pierrots return to the inner rectangle to re-parade the dishes and, as in a game of musical chairs, set them down in new places. The Jellied Seascape is broached and ladled into bowls. Disappointingly, it is a textureless, semi-solid mass studded with pieces of scallop, its flavour interesting but bland after the vigour of the preceding dishes.

Now it is interval. Plates are cleared from tables, wines poured. Once more the musicians are heard, softly; they had been almost forgotten during the excitement of eating. Again, there is a muffled roll of drums. Chairs are hurriedly occupied and the parade of the second service begins. Carried aloft comes the platter of sliced roast suckling pig, crowned by the grinning head; then a large whole snapper, poached in rice wine. Two Pierrots invite us to peer into a brown-glazed lattice basket, woven from strands of bread dough. In it lie pieces of goose and venison. Another platter passes, bearing the Mount of Pigeons, crisp and dark-skinned, supporting each other like a pyramid of circus acrobats.

We applaud in admiration of these, and of the final platter, the magician's trick of quails cooked in bladders – little balloons that hold juices and aroma captive. Less distanced now, the Pierrots are almost participating in our banquet. One Pierrot, inexpertly slitting open a bladder to remove a tiny bird, finds voice to comment. Others ask us, at the second tour of the dishes, whether we would like a piece of goose or venison, a serving of snapper. Finding them less formidable, we make so bold as to request a spoon of sauce, a slice of suckling pig.

The second interval is more animated, more relaxed. The order is fading; guests stand in groups to chat or form small, intimate circles of chairs. Voices become louder and looser, visions blur, gestures become more reckless. We help ourselves to more wine, while some of the Pierrots mingle with the guests. The cooks themselves, all too human in greasy T-shirts, make brief appearances and accept congratulations. Indeed, the banquet structure is so far eroded that dessert seems to arrive unheralded, and is borne in by a Pierrot assisted by an ordinary mortal. It is a guest who comes to the rescue as the red-and-white carnival cone of ice cream starts to slide off its base. On another tray is a rough-and-tumble pile of fresh raspberries, encircled by tall *cigarettes-russes* cones, while a large slab of glass supports the mirror-surfaced expanse of blackberry trifle. There is no formality with dessert; it is each to his own now. One of the guests locates the coffee machine and starts coffee, another opens and offers an ice cold Tokay.

Slowly, the evening winds down. Addresses are exchanged, farewells kissed. The ballroom is in disorder, with chairs scattered, dishes piled up for washing, dessert leftovers here and there, an almost untouched plate of chocolates and nougat among unfinished cups of coffee. The performance over, cooks and Pierrots discard their roles and gather in a corner for their backstage party. Reluctantly, we go our separate ways, promising to meet tomorrow.

This was no ordinary banquet, its form dictated by protocol, but an original production designed to serve as a spectacular finale to a symposium of gastronomy. The extravaganza of Phillip Searle and Cheong Liew was a response to the tag of 'upstart', this first Symposium of Australian Gastronomy in 1984 having adopted as its theme Gay Bilson's remark that this is 'an upstart culinary country', a land as devoid of culinary tradition as of water. This pessimistic theme was elaborated during the formal sessions: we have no gastronomic heritage, having severed the connection between agriculture and eating, and having failed, from the very beginning, to take advantage of the knowledge and experience of the indigenous population; we have no gastronomic quality, our fruits and vegetables being selected primarily for their colour and durability; we have no tradition of gastronomic writing, because writing about food and eating is considered frivolous. To such negative attitudes, the banquet came as a positive and practical response.

First was the menu, bold and up-front. Not only was it in direct contrast to the abstract theorising of earlier papers and discussions, but it mischievously created discord. Each dish was described in simple, stark terms (Suckling Pig; A Basket of Goose and Venison), deliberate understatements that were at variance with the fashionable verbosity of nouvelle cuisine. Moreover, the mental images evoked by the menu descriptions were at odds with the reality of the dishes presented. No one could have conceived of 'Steamed Lambs' Brains' as individual domes under the palest, translucent green cover, nor 'Raspberry and Vanilla Icecream' as an outsize cone of alternate spirals of pink and white, nor 'Goose Liverwurst' as a massive, black block over which was draped a greyish, phallic sausage.

And the dishes themselves were bold and assertive, a glorious celebration of food and eating in true Rabelaisian spirit. They evoked

•

•

a medieval Carnival feast, the orgy of flesh-eating before the piously monotonous fish-and-legume days of Lent. At this banquet there was no lamb, beef or chicken, none of the everyday foods, but rather goose, venison, quail, pigeon, suckling pig – exceptional, extravagant ingredients symbolising the rich and conspicuous consumption that characterises the feast. There were no vegetables, not even a salad, to interrupt the succession of flesh-based dishes. Continuing the medieval analogy was the platter of suckling pig surmounted by the whole head, mouth agape as if in mocking laughter, eyes heaven-fixed, which was reminiscent of the boar's head of medieval banquets, traditionally borne in by a succession of domestics to a fanfare of trumpets. There was the Mount of Pigeons, waiting to be attacked and dismembered with sticky fingers, and the allegory of milky-white quail, untimely torn from the soft bladder-wombs, innocent to the tips of their pink-translucent claws.

Then the clowns, not the tumbling, laughter-producing clowns of the circus, but shadowy and inscrutable Pierrots. The prototype Pierrot, created in the nineteenth century by the French actor Deburau, retained some of the idiosyncrasies of the old Commedia dell'Arte character, Harlequin – such as his sense of mischief – but Deburau's dominant characteristic was a speechless, almost faceless, sarcasm. His Pierrot could make fun of anything and everything without passion and without speech. At this banquet, the Pierrots acted as detached commentators. They were dissociated from the main action – eating, drinking and talking – but acted as intermediaries between the guests-as-performers and the guests-as-audience, facilitating these Janus-like roles. They reversed the customary master–servant relationship and held power over the guests. Freed from conventional morality, they could express thoughts and feelings usually held in check. They frowned on abstinence and encouraged drinking; they showed disgust at the goose liverwurst sausage; they used their fingers for serving. They could display mockery rather than respect, scorn rather than envy, ridicule rather than reverence.

The clown, equally at home in the worlds of reality and of the imagination, symbolises the creative artist. These Pierrots emphasised that this banquet was no mere meal but a total artistic experience: *la fête, la festa*, the special-occasion feast that delights and stimulates all the senses. It was a spectacular event, a 'spectacle' in the French sense. The philosopher Rousseau, in his famous 'Lettre à M. d'Alembert sur les Spectacles' offered his ideas for *'la fête'*: *'Donnez les spectateurs en spectacle,'* he wrote: *'Rendez-les acteurs eux-mêmes; faites que chacun se voie et s'aime dans les autres, afin que tous en soient mieux unis.'* (Put the spectators in the spectacle. Make them actors themselves; make each see himself and love himself in the others in order that all become one.)

Seated around the outer periphery of the rectangle, we realised, in part, Rousseau's suggestion, and became aware that we were not only audience but performers. Looking up from eating, across the void to the table opposite, we saw our reflections in the act of eating. It was as if we were in the simultaneous positions of voyeur and actor, image and object, active and passive. We could see ourselves greedily attacking and passionately consuming the foods on our plates and, at the same time, as detached observers we could perceive our own cruelty.

For there is an aspect of cruelty in eating, nourishing one life at the expense of another. It is an aspect usually avoided – the crudeness of a slab of blood-red meat is disguised by cooking it, camouflaging it with sauces and garnishes. At this banquet little attempt was made to hide the crudeness and cruelty. Few of the dishes were 'pretty', like colour illustrations in cookbooks and glossy magazines, nor were they the Japanese-influenced works of art of nouvelle cuisine. The sausage of goose liverwurst had an appearance of flesh-coloured, shiny plastic; the solid block of the same was encrusted with jagged pieces of truffle, like broken glass on prison walls. The large poached snapper, grey and lifeless, was arranged in swimming position, its teeth bared and vicious; the pyramid of pigeons resembled a funeral pyre. Such dishes defied consumption rather than invited it and yet, faithful gourmands that we were, we consumed them.

Now, twelve years on, this banquet has achieved cult status. It marked, as did the inauguration of the series of Symposiums of Australian Gastronomy, a new phase of confidence in the gastronomic future of this country. It contributed enormously to the debate on Australian cuisine and Australia's culinary identity. It was an upstart banquet, a new and revitalised form reshaping past traditions. It forced us to think again about food and eating, about the relationships between production and consumption and about the place of gastronomy in the world order. And not least, it caused us to reflect on the art and craft of the cook and the double nature of the cook's chosen medium, for food not only satisfies material appetites but also expresses powerful and subtle ideas.

METAMORPHOSES

OF THE BANQUET

The final service was followed by an impromptu dance by the cook and all his assistants, some carrying torches, others their pots and pans and bells.

IN A LONG, UPSTAIRS gallery of the Musée Lorrain in Nancy, France, there is a series of five tapestries that once would have graced a lord's palace. Hung in the great hall where state receptions were held, the tapestries would have silently reproached any guest who enjoyed himself too much. They depict scenes from a northern French

•

•

morality play written in the late fifteenth century, *La Condamnation de Banquet*. The first three show elegant young noblemen happily eating and drinking with their hosts, the personified *Dîner* (Dinner), *Souper* (Supper) and *Banquet*. Having dined and supped in the first two tapestries, the merry group of revellers – rejoicing in such names as *Gourmandise, Friandise, Bonne Compagnie* (Good Company), *Passe-Temps* (Leisure) – are led on, by *Banquet*, to a real banquet, where rich and sumptuous foods are arrayed on a long table for the guests to help themselves, without the intrusion of servants.

Unbeknown to the guests, however, the double-crossing *Banquet* and *Souper* have plotted to have the guests attacked by a plague of personified maladies – including Apoplexy, Pleurisy, Colic and Gout – and only three guests survive.these three bring an indignant case before Dame Experience, who is aided by four doctors: Hippocrates, Galen, Avicenna and Averroes, names that would have been well known to medieval audiences. *Souper* and *Banquet* are arrested and tried, and both found guilty. *Banquet* is executed and *Souper* is ordered to keep a respectable distance from *Dîner*. The moral is clear.

In the fifteenth century the banquet was a new form of festivity. The word 'banquet' itself dates from that time, derived from the Italian *banchetto*, a long bench or table. This allegory indicates that it was seen by some as a corrupting influence, introducing undesirable values and practices at odds with those promoted by Church authorities. It seems to have begun as a specifically secular celebration, the 'feast' being more closely associated with religious celebrations, a special meal eaten on a feast day: the Sunday dinner and the meals commemorating Easter, Christmas and saints' days. The new banquet was not ritualised and observed no such regularity. It developed more as an individual celebration, often a demonstration of wealth and power in an example of conspicuous consumption. Lavish and large scale, it apparently diverged from other festive meals – why else would a new word be necessary?

The banquet's origins are in early Renaissance Italy. As Italian artistic and culinary influence spread northwards in the fifteenth and sixteenth centuries, so did the banquet. The French term '*banquet*' and Spanish '*banquete*' were both borrowed from the Italian, and the French term was subsequently adopted by the English early in the sixteenth century. The diffusion of the banquet was helped by the installation of Italian artists, architects, sculptors (and even cooks) in French courts. In 1516 François I invited Leonardo da Vinci to his château at Amboise, where the artist helped design costumes for spectacular outdoor *fêtes* in the palace grounds, high above the Loire.

The difference, in the beginning, was in the style and presentation. The various dishes, chosen for their visual impact, were set out on a long table, as depicted in the third tapestry and as a buffet would be arrayed today. In France it seems to have been a supplementary meal, offered late in the evening after the two standard meals of dinner, around midday, and supper in the early evening. Olivier de la Marche has described how the fad spread through northern France in the mid-fifteenth century, and how this novel form of feasting, at first relatively simple, developed into a much grander celebration, more ostentatious and costly, as each nobleman who offered a banquet tried to outdo the previous one. In England, the banquet was not so much a differentiated meal as an elaboration of what had previously been the final course of a formal dinner, the dessert. It was separate to the other courses of a dinner and even served in a different setting. According to historian Anne Wilson, the gentry often built special banqueting houses in their parks, or the guests would withdraw to another room of the mansion, an outside arbour or a summerhouse.

This development was several steps removed from Italian banquets which, by the early sixteenth century, had become spectacular events celebrating the arrival or departure of a prince (often associated with the dramatic ritual of a procession), or a marriage that united noble and/or wealthy families. In his sixteenth-century manual of banquet-giving, *Banchetti, Composizione di vivande et apparecchio generale* (1549) Christoforo di Messisbugo describes, in unparalled detail, the management and staging of ceremonial banquets, starting with the setting of the tables with several tablecloths and ornamental figures of sugar or marzipan, and including instructions for the accompanying music and the dances to be performed during the meal. For example, at a dinner in 1529 for don Ercole, son of the duke of Ferrara, Messisbugo had craftsmen create a sugar model of Hercules and the lion, coloured and gilded, to decorate the table (and incidentally, symbolise strength and power). With the final course of '*confetti*' (sugared spices) came more sugar models representing Venus, Cupid, Eve and other mythical figures. Messisbugo details the musical and vocal entertainments for each course, and the performance of the clowns later in the meal. At another dinner, this time in a garden setting, the table was graced by large sugar figures, all gilded and painted, representing Venus, Bacchus and Cupid.

The banquet was born in an era of culinary innovation, and it offered the cook opportunities to display skill, art and imagination. In Italy, by the mid-fifteenth century, the technique of clarifying jellies with egg whites had been mastered and the arts of marzipan and of

●

●

sugar confectionery had been learnt from the Arabs. The emphasis on culinary ornamentation was a natural corollary. Sugar was still an expensive ingredient, loaded with prestige, and thus appropriate to any festivity. A French banquet menu of 1495 shows a reckless use of sugar in such dishes as 'chickens with sugar', 'quails with sugar', 'pigeons with sugar and vinegar'. In England, too, sugar featured strongly in banquet foods – fruit tarts, marmalades, preserves, marzipan and jelly – all accompanied by sweet wines, and all highly decorative. Gervase Markham, in his cookery book of 1615, *The English Hus-wife*, includes a separate chapter on 'Banqueting and made dishes with other conceits and secrets' where he gives recipes for these very dishes.

Superficially, Messisbugo's extravaganzas might be seen as representing merely a refinement of earlier medieval practices. In noble and aristocratic circles, medieval feasts also featured music and dance in the 'entremets' – literally, something that came between courses. These could have been as fantastic as a pastry castle with singers and musicians in each of its towers. At a splendiferous feast offered to Pope Clement VI at Avignon by Cardinal Hannibal Ceccano in the mid-fourteenth century, the nine courses were punctuated by several entremets, all products of the kitchen but, like margarine sculptures today, not necessarily made to be eaten. There was an enormous castle apparently constructed of deers, wild boars, hares and rabbits, all cooked but looking very much alive. Pheasants, peacocks and swans, again cooked but redressed in all their plumage, surrounded a fountain from which flowed three different kinds of wine. All these were paraded around the room to the accompaniment of music. The final service consisted of two 'trees', one said to be of silver, both laden with all kinds of fruits representing the pinnacle of the confectioner's art. The presentation of these 'trees' was followed by an impromptu dance by the cook and all his assistants, some carrying torches, others their pots and pans and bells.

Such between-course spectaculars were typically the product of the kitchen, elaborated under the charge of the head cook. Maistre Chiquart, cook to the Count of Savoy, gave 'recipes' for the preparation and construction of amazing decorative pieces in his cookery book of 1420. Other books included recipes for pies of the four-and-twenty blackbirds genre, explaining how to bake a pastry case with a lift-off lid (the secret was to fill the pastry case, before baking, with flour, emptying it out later through a purpose-built hole in the side).

In the banquet's evolution the culinary and theatrical elements became separated. The entremets as spectacle became almost purely theatrical – music, mime, dance, and acrobatics – leaving cooks free to devote all their skills to food and its visual display. Gervase Markham is quite explicit; 'banquetting stuff' may not be 'of general use, yet in their true times they are so needful for adornation'. As a total art form, the banquet probably reached its apogee in the seventeenth century, when Louis XIV entertained on a grandiose scale at Versailles, and when Inigo Jones designed the Banqueting House in Whitehall, with its Rubens ceilings depicting romanticised scenes from the life of James I.

Then came the Revolution in France, and a new style of banquet: the *banquet civique* or public banquet, a communal meal intended to celebrate a famous anniversary or victory. Like the Renaissance banquet, public banquets were conceived on a vast scale and accompanied by music, dance and visual spectacle, but unlike the former they were not restricted to the nobility. One of the leaders of the

•

•

Revolution, a few days after the taking of the Bastille, called for a national *fête* to mark the date of the uprising. 'Our revolution had no precedents, and we have no example to follow; we need a new form of celebration,' he wrote.

> *I would like all the citizens of Paris to set up their tables outside, in front of their houses, and eat in the street. Rich would mix with poor, all the social classes would be united. The streets would be hung with carpets, garlanded with flowers; no one would be allowed to traverse the streets, either on horseback or in a carriage. From one end of the capital to the other we would be one immense family; there would be a million people at the one table; toasts would be drunk, to the peal of bells from all the churches, to the sound of a volley of canons and muskets, orchestrated simultaneously in all parts of the city; on that day, the nation will have its grand couvert.*

In the Musée Carnavalet in Paris, you can see realistic depictions of these public banquets, painted by contemporary artists in naïve style. They were quite popular in France in the eighteenth century, although they disappeared in the nineteenth during the Restoration. The gastronomic philosopher Brillat-Savarin seems to have been inspired by such events in the celebration he imagined for Gastéréa's special day (September 21), which similarly included a mass, open-air feast followed by music and dancing. Like the Revolutionaries, he, too, was seeking a new form of festivity for a new society.

The public banquet, it was soon realised, could also be used for political purposes, and the French *banquets réformistes* of the mid-nineteenth century ensured that propaganda replaced celebration, oratory replaced music. In nineteenth-century England, and also in

Australia and America, the banquet developed as a formal and official state celebration ritualised with toasts and speeches. *The Banquet Book*, published in New York in 1902, is subtitled: 'A Classified Collection of Quotations Designed for General Reference, and also as an Aid in the Preparation of the Toast List, the After-Dinner Speech, and the Occasional Address; together with Suggestions concerning the Menu and certain other Details connected with the proper Ordering of the Banquet.' Curiously, the English-inspired menus of official Australian banquets, such as the 1888 banquet celebrating the first hundred years of colonisation and the 1897 Federal Convention banquet, once again make the desserts – or, as they were usually described, the entremets – the high point of the dinner.

Official banquets, with their formal ceremony and state-ordained protocol, are as far from the extravagant Renaissance spectaculars as the ubiquitous 'banquets' offered in Chinese restaurants in Australia – though the lovingly turned carrots and turnip chrysanthemums are an echo of Messisbugo's sugar Cupids. On the other hand, the public banquets celebrating Liberty, Egality and Fraternity in France have multitudinous offspring: the *repas communaux* organised in communes all over the country on July 14. Held in the open air, or under makeshift roofs, they are truly communal, open to everyone for a minimal cost, the whole village pitching in to help with setting up and cooking and serving. And since everyone in a village is more or less distantly related, they have the air of a family picnic, albeit the reunion of a vast extended family. Their long benches and trestle tables hark back to the original banquets, but the message of these modern celebrations is a simple one of communion, the act of sharing.

•

•

BASTILLE DAY AT CLARET

AND ITS 'REPAS COMMUNAL'

Those at table anxiously await the free aperitif — a double slug of pastis in a paper cup, poured by the assistant to Monsieur le Maire whose offsider follows with a large garden watering can and tops up each cup.

14 JULY: BASTILLE DAY, and the start of one of the three main holiday periods in France. In Paris there's a ritual parade along the Champs-Elysées, extravagant fireworks and dancing in the street (*le bal dans la rue,* as celebrated by Edith Piaf) in practically every *quartier.*

•

•

It is also the night of the annual firemen's balls, for which notices are plastered all over the city.

In the villages the celebrations have a character all of their own, often culminating in a *repas communal*, for which an open invitation is extended to everyone in the commune. This one belonged to Claret, an almost forgotten village in the Languedoc. The heart of the village is its square, in which an ancient fountain intermittently spouts fresh spring water. On one side is a simple Roman-style church and on the other the local *mairie*, centre of all information for and about the villagers. Nearby is a leisurely post office, a *café-bar*, a *boulangerie* and a couple of general store-*épiceries*. Narrow, dusty houses surround the square and line the narrow, pedestrian-only streets that radiate from it.

Schools have broken up for the long summer holidays, but for the children this is a special holiday. They are out in the streets early, the boys in their Sunday-best clean shirts and ironed pants, the girls with ribbons in their hair and wearing long, little-girl dresses. The bakery and general stores open for a morning's hectic business, since the day merits a special dinner with Sunday treats of glazed pastries and fruit tarts and a tray of enormous peaches. The men, standing together in small groups in the square, are also in their Sunday best. The women, as usual, are busy in their kitchens. Just before midday a straggly procession of men makes its way to the *Mairie*, unearths a few *drapeaux tricolores* and a dusty wreath, and files off to the *Monument aux Morts* to get the official part of the day over and done with, before eating and playing.

The highlight of the day, and prelude to the evening's entertainment, is to be a *Concours de Boules*, and in a progressive gesture the men have announced a bowls competition for women, too – as long as there are at least four teams willing to play. Playing wherever there's clear space, level or not – on the dirt under the plane trees, the gravel around the church, the bitumenised road outside the *épicerie* (where due care has been taken to cover the hole at the end of the open drain) – the men and women draw a crowd, and children set up their own games alongside, using child-size bowls. By seven o'clock the women have finished their competition (won by Madame *l'épicière*, daughter of our landlady) and have returned home to change into something more appropriate to the evening's festivity. The children, somewhat grubbier, are livening up in anticipation.

An amateur band arrives and starts rehearsing. It's a local band, with an odd assembly of traditional instruments: a violin; a set of bagpipes, smaller and more peasantish than the Scottish ones; a high-pitched, almost oriental-sounding Provençal fife; a flat, sitar-like stringed instrument; a set of bells on the legs of the man with the bag-pipes; and a *vielle*, or hurdy-gurdy. The man with the *vielle* has continual problems with breaking strings and eventually gives up. The amplification system can't be made to work, either, so the group abandons the makeshift stage for a circle of chairs in the middle of the square. The youth of the village congregate and start dancing in the style they've learnt from television.

Meanwhile, long trestle tables are being set up around three sides of the square and an enormous pile of *sarments* (dried vine prunings) is made ready for the match. Those in the know lay claim to particular seats; we find two places next to the local fisherman (whom we had sat next to at the inaugural meeting of the local branch of the Socialist Party, an event celebrated with unfortunately warm champagne) and a twinkle-eyed patriarch who gleefully tells us how he's managed to leave his wife at home. As they place their knives, forks and serviettes on the table we are reminded that this is a bring-your-own affair (it costs no more than the equivalent of six baguettes), and we dash back for implements.

Like the bowls competition, now triumphantly concluded (the winners are still at the Café des Sports), the *repas communal* is behind schedule. The manager of the *Cave Coopérative* has taken over administration of the bonfire and quickly has it flaming high. His acolytes prepare an enormous grid on which the dinner will cook. Those at table anxiously await the free aperitif – a double slug of pastis in a paper cup, poured by the assistant to *Monsieur le Maire*, whose offsider follows with a large garden watering can and tops up each cup. At last the first course arrives – paper plates of ham, sausage, pâté, olives and chunks of bread. Volunteers rake hot coals under the grids and throw on strings of fat pork sausages and hot, spicy North African *merguez*. Wives are called in to help, handing out more bread, handfuls of potato chips, jars of mustard. The handsome *Cave Coopérative* man wheels around a barrowful of bottles of the local vintage, one bottle for every two participants, and the assistant to the *Maire* distributes the sausages and merguez equitably, one of each per person. Everyone eats and drinks.

The band does too, so the square is filled with the sounds of eating and wine-amplified voices. More wine is broached and passed around, and we listen, enthralled, to tales of the village and the fish that got away and, for the umpteenth time, of the wife who was left at home. As evening settles, foil-wrapped triangles of Vache-qui-rit cheese are offered, and large fresh peaches. However makeshift, this meal follows to the letter the standard French formula. Sensing the mood, the band starts up again with a simple, rhythmical chorus that attracts pairs of young girls and, eventually, the grown-ups, in a constantly breaking and re-forming procession that expands and contracts in segments like a giant earthworm. I find myself dancing with Monsieur Poste, lighter on his feet than I ever imagined him on his bicycle. Over there is the lady who sells the *Midi-Libre* from her front room, dreamily dancing with another woman (we discover, next morning, that Madame Midi-Libre has inexplicably disappeared).

At last, the children have had enough and, resting on a shoulder, fall into a dead sleep. The dancers diminish as parents head home with their offspring. Midnight comes, the band is tired, and tomorrow is a normal day. We stroll back to to the house we have rented for the month, exchanging goodnights with the holidaying Parisians as we pass and, languidly climbing the stairs, revel in the warmth of the evening and its company.

A   S U R R E A L I S T   B A N Q U E T ,   1 9 9 3

All art is a revolt against man's fate.
— André Malraux

THE SURREALIST ARTISTS of the 1930s took delight in paradox, in the juxtaposition of the unexpected with the unconventional – whether deliberately to shock and to challenge bourgeois sensibilities, or ingenuously to push back the boundaries of perception and representation. In like fashion, the banquet presented by Gay Bilson, Yanni Kyritsis and the team of Berowra Waters Out for the Seventh Symposium of Australian Gastronomy in Canberra in 1993 confronted diners with images demanding intellectual as well as physiological digestion.

•

1 5 7

•

'Confronted' and 'demanding'. I choose the words deliberately, for this banquet was not for the faint-hearted. It was not one of those easy-going dinners that invite gluttony but rather a 'spectacle', in the Rousseau-ist sense, and as much theatre as gastronomy. And if its intent was to reflect the spirit of the surrealist creations that hung in the gallery above us as we ate, then its interpretation must be sought at the deeper level of symbolic association.

This 1993 exhibition at the National Gallery offered, as an aperitif, two cases of Barry Humphries' dada art, including his Cakescape: squashed lamingtons and slices of jam roll which, unexpectedly, seemed more at home in a frame than on the tea table. The variations of texture and colour in his creations made them quite entrancing – childish, innocuous and superficially appealing. Not so Gay Bilson's introduction to the banquet, which also made use of edible materials. Beneath the harsh glare of surgical lights, we were faced with a long narrow table draped with the stomachs of several large beasts, turned inside out to display surfaces of fine-textured honeycomb and warty protrusions, in colours of dirty beige, muddy brown and brindled black: the guts, in all their glory, as if to say, 'This is where the processes of transformation and incorporation take place; this is the beginning.'

Unexpected? Undoubtedly; and for some, also obscene. But once the connection with animal insides is ignored, the visual effects can be appreciated: the contrast of textures, surfaces that invite a cautious caress, secret orifices. The result is fascination more than revulsion, a fascination that is not merely scientific but includes more than a hint of empathy. We, too, are mortal.

The spectre of mortality overlay this banquet. Not that we were

•

•

constantly faced with a vision of intestines – after the necessary time for seating all the guests, these were neatly rolled up in undertaker's plastic and removed to another place. The table was then set with the conventional implements: glass, knife-fork-spoon laid on a micro-scope slide, carafe of water. For this act, and for the rest of the evening, the waiters discarded their customary white shirts and, with them, their customary role. Bound with a bandage over the right shoulder and around the diaphragm, they became the walking wounded, the battle-scarred, those who have brushed with death and glimpsed the nether world.

No menus were provided to tell us what we should be eating or drinking. We were left with our senses. Surprisingly, the visual sense came to dominate, recognition leading to trust, and trust to tasting. Reliance on sight was such that some dishes were practically untouched – as though the eyes had direct connections to the con-sciousness, which could easily be persuaded that what looked like bull's pizzles actually were . . .

In fact, the banquet began in a fairly conventional fashion with a dish most of us recognised: a nest of raw beef, in short strips, in which sat a raw egg yolk, topped with anchovy fillets, capers and finely chopped onion. We doused it with warmly golden olive oil, and crackled thin, crisp wafers of bread in accompaniment. The consommé, ladled from tall white jugs, appeared equally orthodox – until we discerned the gelatin-richness as it slipped from the ladle, and admired its inten-sity of flavour. With the consommé came a jumbled mass of marrow bones, some gilded with gold leaf. Their core could be spread over the slice of toasted brioche or added to the broth, making glistening circles of fat on its limpid surface.

By the time we received the next dish, crisply fried sheets of fish skin atop token shreds of vegetable, a pattern was emerging. We had eaten flesh, bones, marrow, skin – what next? Almost inevitably, it was blood, in the form of a crisp-coated *boudin* or blood sausage – a very rich and impeccably seasoned *boudin*, accompanied by pan-fried wedges of apple. The wine changed to sparkling burgundy for this course, though all the wines were red, even the blood-tinged *kir royale* which preceded the banquet (the waiters had been given orders not to serve the champagne solo, but only with the *cassis*). Why sparkling burgundy? Perhaps its bubbles were meant to invoke the oxygen-carrying role of blood in the body. Or perhaps the element of cultural sophistication associated with bubbles in the booze was meant to accentuate the crudeness of consuming blood, the very essence of the body, and the paradox of offering this most primitive of foods as part of a formal banquet.

There was more to come: a dish of rare pigeon breast, served on caramel-sweet red cabbage, the whole surrounded by pinkish-brown cones (skewered hearts of duck and pigeon) that looked so like miniature pizzles. And a cheese course: a melting wedge of almost unnaturally fresh cheese, lightly seasoned with pesto, inside puff pastry of buttery ephemerality. I began to long for a salad, vegetables, anything to break the carnal sequence. Instead, we were given a blindfold.

Certainly, the revelation deserved a blindfold; the element of surprise was all-important. But the blindfold also signified a turning point in the meal, as we moved to fruit and cereals, the domain of Demeter, goddess of fertility and mellow fruitfulness. It is Demeter's daughter and alter ego, Persephone, who, after an enforced sojourn in Hades, returns annually to earth for the sowing and harvest. We, too, were condemned to darkness before the re-awakening – to find before us purple figs and black grapes, dark damson jelly and firm white cream, glazed yeast cakes topped with juicy grapes and, in the centre of the table, a bandage-swathed young girl, covered in figs and grapes.

This was no nubile Lolita leaping out of a chocolate heart. As she stiffly raised her head and shoulders from the table, I saw her as the Life that succeeds Death – that same Death that had attracted the funerary tributes heaped about her. On the eternal roundabout, she was both Life and Death, transformed from the dead to the living by the offerings of fruit and bread. This banquet was a celebration of Life through Death, a reminder of our fate to be born, to die, to be recycled.

With coffee, too, came Life and Death, as if to affirm this natural sequence: Virgin's Breasts (moulded almond cakes with glazed nipples) and Dead Men's Bones (thin, crisp, pale brown biscuits). Eating these, we incorporated both future and past in our own present, absorbing them into our bodies which, metaphorically as well as physiologically, include these three dimensions.

Shocking as it was to some, Gay Bilson's banquet could not have been designed simply to jolt us out of complacency. Nor could it have been merely a joke on us, gluttons all to some extent, and greedy for the next and newest taste sensation. Its significance must lie else-where – not only in surrealism, but also in the theme of the sympo-sium, Nature and Culture.

Culture is often seen as corrupting of innocent Nature, and cookery is an application of Culture. (This was the view of the cynic Diogenes, who shunned cooked food and, indeed, all forms of civili-sation.) Physically, we were on the side of Culture – inside an art gallery, separated by plate glass from the garden and gum trees outside. The foods we were served represented the basest of Nature – viscera, bones, blood – transformed by culinary artists in a demonstration of the triumph of Culture. And this transformation was necessary; in their natural form, few of us could have stomached such ingredients. This banquet was an affirmation of the relevance of Culture to our lives.

But I saw it, too, as a form of sacrament, as much a sacrament as the supper of bread and wine. It contained all the elements of ancient worship and sacrifice to the Gods – though we were not witness to the ascent of the aromatic smoke. Its carnality (emphasised by the serving of red wine only) spoke also of primal rituals.

This affinity with ancient religion underlined the transience of life and inexorability of Fate, and accentuated the theme of mortality that ran throughout the entire banquet. And, given that a banquet is a formalised and celebratory occasion for eating and drinking, this is perhaps the ultimate paradox.

FOOD AND PERFORMANCE,

FOOD IN PERFORMANCE

Cooking itself is performance, as all serious cooks know instinctively, and anyone knows who has watched, entranced, as the pizza cook tosses the dough, spreads and garnishes it as though he had the six arms of an Indian goddess.

IT IS ENTIRELY APPROPRIATE, given theatre's somewhat louche origins in the singing, dancing, feasting and carrying-on in the name of Dionysus – and remember, before being honoured with the wine portfolio, this rotund, grape-festooned character was merely in charge

•

•

of harvests and fertility – that food and cooking and eating should still have a role on the stage. Usually, it's as an accessory, as in a performance of David Williamson's play, *Travelling North*, where the spitting and sizzling of chops and sausages on a portable barbecue, and their utterly unambiguous aroma, greeted the audience returning after interval and told them, before their eyes had even glimpsed the set, that they were in a suburban Australian backyard.

Food and performance should touch at many points. In the ancient festivals of Dionysus, where the visual spectacle of the procession served as a prelude to contests in comedy and tragedy, food and wine fuelled the exuberance of the participants in celebratory song and dance. These festivals themselves were civilised and politically-correct versions of older and more primitive food-centred rituals, where the god of vegetation and fertility was feted and flattered in the hope of ensuring the earth's abundance for another year.

The tradition of communal feasting has gone out of fashion in most modern western societies, where the emphasis is on the individual, but in trans-Caucasian Georgia – where perhaps there's more respect for community solidarity – it seems to have kept an important social and celebratory significance. As with most rituals, it is participatory, and music is as important an ingredient as food and wine. Its explicit purpose is to unite the guests around one table, no matter how long the table or how many corners it turns. At this endless table the guests eat, drink and sing in unison traditional table songs, polyphonic chants with origins almost as old as the vine and viticulture (which probably began in Georgia, too). There is unity of action, under the direction of the toastmaster who announces each toast, and specific rules govern the feast, including penalties for those caught

•

•

eating, drinking or singing at the wrong time. Particular toasts are associated with particular songs, and some must be proposed with a particular food – the obligatory toast to the dead must be offered at the time of the meat course.

The Renaissance banquet may have taken inspiration from the Dionysian festivities, following a different evolutionary path to become a multi-media participatory spectacle based on, and expressed through, food. In sixteenth- and seventeenth-century Europe, the golden age of banqueting, these spectacles brought together the arts of the cook, the carver, the musician, the dancer, the performer – and the eater. Guests at these events were expected to behave in accordance with a certain code; they, too, were acting their parts, following an internalised script.

Like theatre, the banquet often had an ulterior motive beyond mere entertainment. It was used to encourage political solidarity, to impress and honour distinguished guests, to demonstrate wealth, power and status. For any of these purposes, the various arts could be called upon to reinforce the message. Sugar and marzipan sculptures, allegorically costumed dancers, mythology-based mimes: with the hindsight of several centuries such artistic creations appear quite blatantly didactic. If these elements were so effective in entertaining and informing the assemblage, why then was it was thought necessary to construct the spectacle around food?

The answer – apart from the fact that these banquets represented the continuance of an ancient tradition – is that it would have been impossible to achieve the same overall effect with a variety night: food is fundamental. Food is absorbed, literally incorporated; it enters via all the senses, taking its symbolic properties with it. Eating and

•

•

drinking engender a feeling of well-being, both physical and spiritual. Finally, food has a social function; eating together is an expression of conviviality. Regardless of social differences (again, clearly expressed through food, its quality and quantity), banquet guests were united by being participants at the same feast. As participants, they influenced its direction and its unfolding, and were integrated into the performance. While the music, song and dance were complementary accessories, without the food the event would have been but a shadow of itself.

In all rituals – and whatever their purpose, rituals are staged events – food and drink have major roles, whether destined for deities or human consumption, or both. Yet in the evolution of the Dionysian festival, drama took a divergent path to focus more on narrative and visual aesthetics, at the same time distancing itself from food and separating performers from audience. As a result, the connections between food and theatre are today typically unacknowledged, and rarely exploited – though perhaps this also has something to do with the fact that theatre, in the cultural hierarchy, enjoys a more exalted position than food.

On occasions theatre relies on social and cultural food associations to add layers of meaning to plot and character. I remember a performance by the Georgian Film Actors' Studio of *Bacula's Pig*, which described the head-on confrontations in a small, traditional Georgian community when a Russian official is sent to administer and enforce the (Russian) law. Seemingly defeated by the overwhelming rationality of the bureaucracy, the villagers, in a spirit of generosity and conciliation, invite the official to a Georgian feast honouring some local custom. As Act II opens, the table is set with jugs of wine – but the

•

•

official, arriving in his Russian fur hat and military greatcoat, initially asks for vodka, thereby betraying his 'otherness'. Gradually, having consumed the roast chicken, under the spell of the wine and infused by song, he loses his Russian character, and affirms his affinity with Georgia by calling for more wine, swapping coat and hat with one of the locals and joining in a rousing dance. Hardly subtle, in terms of symbolism, but forceful in effect.

In the same way the film *Babette's Feast* showed how a whole village, previously suspicious, hostile and divided, could be reunited around the table. Stiffly formal and almost mute at first, the guests sip cautiously of dishes that they have resolved not to eat but, such is the persuasive power of the food and wine, soon start to enjoy. They share dishes, clink glasses and, at the close of the meal, are once more a community of friends, generous, forgiving and understanding of one another. Using food to convey or enhance a message is apparently easier (and more law-abiding) in film than on the stage, for several recent films in recent years have given food a starring role – *The Cook, The Thief, His Wife and Her Lover* and *Like Water for Chocolate* are notable examples.

In the traditional trilogy of performance arts, drama shares the stage with music and dance. In the newer offshoot simply described as 'performance', the three are often integrated and combined. Performance tends to be characterised by spontaneity and improvisation. It does not depend on stage, set and auditorium but can happen anywhere – in the street, in the middle of a room – with the result that the line between performers and audience blurs, and the audience might even be absorbed into the piece. Unlike theatre, where actors speak words written by someone else under the direction of another in a set designed by yet another member of the team, performance is usually the product of a single individual who devises, produces and performs the piece – or of a collaborative group, which together does the same thing.

The performance genre rejects many of the formalised conventions of theatre and frequently has little interest in telling a story, preferring to communicate ideas, experiences and emotions. The traditional Georgian feast is itself a kind of performance. More than traditional theatre, performance has affinities with the ritual, a participatory event that necessarily involves the consumption and sharing of food and drink. Performance explores the possibilities associated with food which, because of its powerful symbolic associations and because it touches all the senses, is a persuasive messenger and finds in performance a felicitous medium. Given the personal and often autobiographical nature of performance pieces, the inclusion of food and drink seems a totally natural way of communication, enhancing the meaning and enriching the experience. Significantly, in most performances the food is no mere pasteboard prop but solid, real and treated with proper respect.

Just as food can be a means of heightening the theatrical experience, so borrowings from theatre heighten the eating experience. Restaurateurs and caterers often conceive their events as performances, mindful of setting, props and lighting. Food writers and restaurant critics regularly borrow metaphors from theatre when describing dining experiences. Cooking itself is performance, as all serious cooks know instinctively, and anyone knows who has watched, entranced, as the pizza cook tosses the dough, spreads and garnishes it as though he had the six arms of an Indian goddess. We applaud the cook's performance as she deftly manoeuvres the pans over the flames, turning here and tossing there and swapping this one with that with all the skills of a juggler-cum-puppeteer; we admire the finesse of the maître d over the spirit burner of a silver service restaurant; and we appreciate the graceful movements of sugar-pulling, as the luminously opaque mass is stretched and twisted until it looks for all the world like a fleshier version of one of Giacometti's anguished figures.

Incorporating aspects of food and cooking and eating into performance is relatively simple. Borrowing from theatre to enhance food and cooking and eating is similarly easy – we even talk of 'staging' a banquet. But given the task of making a performance out of food and eating – in other words, a meal – where and how do you start? At a conference at the Cardiff-based Centre for Performance Research, Alicia Rios began by transforming the audience into participants whose role was to harvest lunch inside an imaginary greenhouse. First, we were to enter the greenhouse and walk between the benches that ran along the length of its make-believe walls, observing, wondering and reflecting. On exit, from the opposite end, we were to collect our tools – a miniature wooden-handled rake, digging fork and trowel – plus a plate, then repeat the progression through the greenhouse, this time harvesting our needs on the way. Some of the plants, we were directed, would need 'fertiliser' – and to this end, brightly-coloured watering cans filled with olive oil dressings were left at strategic locations. In case the performers themselves needed fertilising, other, much larger, watering cans held wine.

They were real foods, natural foods, but in the illusory greenhouse they were also performers, acting their allotted roles. As Alicia

•

1 6 9

•

explained, 'This is a game in which the product looks like the real thing without actually being it'. The spectacle of Nature imitating Nature produced a curious mental disorientation, like the play within the play, the image within the image. As in a real greenhouse, the 'plants' were arranged in families, and for the benefit of the botanically inept among us, large signs behind the pots indicated the groupings. First were the cacti: small black plastic containers in neat rows, each one growing a 'cactus' – in reality, an assortment of pickled vegetables (onions, gherkins, olives, peppers) impaled on a toothpick. Next were 'fungi' – mushrooms erupting from a rich brown compost (of coffee dregs); and 'salads', small whole lettuces. Beneath the label 'root vegetables' were large pots containing whole potatoes and carrots, which had to be dug from their 'soil' of cooked brown rice (the same soil which sustained the cacti). Further on were 'aquatics', represented by pale clumps of celery, and 'bonsai', miniature green broccoli shrubs.

The plant kingdom ended abruptly with the Bouquet of Dried Flowers, the most arresting element of the set. It marked a change of direction for the second act: the natural was now represented by the artificial, the 'flowers' composed of the kinds of foods furthest removed from Nature, those garishly coloured snack foods typically described as 'junk'. In this context, however, their base associations vanished before their significance. Flowers they were called, flowers they resembled and, for all intents and purposes, flowers they were. The artificialising of Nature continued with pebbles, mushrooms, miniature snakes which might well have been pretending to be glow-worms, rosy-pink strawberries and lumps of coal, all products of the confectioner's art.

As we ate our lunch in the imaginary greenhouse, with birds chirping and warbling around us (or rather, symbolic birds, their songs only), and from time to time being 'sprayed' with a fine mist of orange-flower water, we were all unconsciously 'performing' – under Alicia's direction – 'A Temperate Menu'. As we ate, we had cause to reflect on the chain of events that form the food cycle, and to question our pre-conceptions concerning the nature of the edible and non-edible. The very acts of harvesting food, preparing it and eating it had been turned into a performance in which there was no audience but only per-formers – or rather, audience and performers were one and the same.

Food in performance, food as performance: the synergetic poten-tial of the combination is boundless.

ON GASTRONOMY

If you go to Byzantium, he advised, 'get a slice of sword-fish,
the joint cut right from the tail'.

LA GASTRONOMIE: *la connaissance raisonnée de tout ce qui a rapport à l'homme en tant qu'il se nourrit.*

GASTRONOMY: the reasoned understanding of everything that concerns us, insofar as we sustain ourselves. – (Brillat-Savarin)

Brillat-Savarin's words roll so glibly off the tongue that we feel absolved from pursuing a further, and personal, understanding. In his succinct definition he encompassed all the specific and multifarious aspects of gastronomy which, at one time or another, are proposed. We need not bother to ask why gastronomy might be important, both to us as individuals and to society as a whole.

At a particular time of the year, when Duchess pears are fresh and ripe and juicy, I like to partner them with certain blue cheeses – Gorgonzola in particular, but Australian Gippsland and Unity blue cheeses are also good. To eat the two together is one of my ritual delights. When the combination succeeds the effect is more than the simple sum of the two constituents. On the other hand, roquefort, also a blue-vein cheese, goes better with fresh walnuts. Why? And is it important to wonder why?

The debate around the dinner table was intense. For some, it was enough that the taste was right, that the combination was pleasurable, that a perfect harmony had been momentarily achieved. Others felt this attitude was akin to the typical 'I don't know much about art/music/theatre but I know what I like', and indicated a certain stolid conservatism. They maintained that sensory enjoyment can be enhanced by going beyond the tasting experience to include an intellectual component, a reflection on the reasons for a particular partnership or the history of a particular food. So diametrically opposed were the two sides that no agreement was possible.

Gastronomy, it seems to me, is at the confluence of the streams of sensuality and intellect. It implies the meeting of mind and body which is the ideal of many religions. Brillat-Savarin, for one, envisaged gastronomy as a kind of religion, a way of life. This aspect is epitomised in the phrase, *'la connaissance raisonnée'* the application of of logic and rationality to the immediacy of sensory images and impressions. Reason moderates the understanding gained through the senses, which themselves nuance intellectual knowledge. For *'connaissance'*

●

●

denotes more than mere erudition, book learning and cold hard facts; it incorporates intuition, warm, soft and sensuous understanding. It is no coincidence that Brillat-Savarin began his Gastronomical Meditations with two chapters on the senses in general and on the sense of taste in particular.

While this might enlighten us, it still does not explain what gastronomy is. And debates persist as to whether gastronomy is a science (the reason part) or an art (the sensory part), or both simultaneously; whether it simply relates to the acts of eating and drinking, or whether it is a far-reaching discipline that encompasses everything into which food enters, from the structure of society to global food politics. Humbled and hesitant, we resist proposing or endorsing a definition of gastronomy, as if the subject were too vast and vague to be so circumscribed. By default we quote the stock phrase borrowed from Brillat-Savarin, explaining that gastronomy has to do with anything and everything that concerns us insofar as we sustain ourselves – thus embracing all aspects of food and drink production, preparation, politics, commerce, trade, marketing, cooking and serving, together with meals and manners and a good many other related topics, all treated in a no-holds-barred fashion that ignores territorial boundaries. I'm not sure that Brillat-Savarin actually meant gastronomy to be quite so extensive, though he did note its pertinence to natural history, physics, chemistry, cookery, commerce and political economy.

Brillat-Savarin's formal definition is somewhat at odds with common usage. When people talk of the gastronomy of Italy, or of China, we know immediately that they are referring to the foods and drinks of those countries, together with the eating and cooking and social traditions that go with them. The qualifier 'gastronomic' is also easily understood. There is no disputing an interpretation of gastronomic heritage as the ensemble of sites, structures and traditions associated with the producing and preparing (and consuming) of food and drink; of gastronomic tourism as tourism focused on eating and drinking; of a gastronomic world-view as a perspective on the world that gives pride of place to the centrality of food production and consumption. Gastronomic literature is understood as reflective writing on food, and eating, and drinking. Gastronomic history is similarly accepted as a particular approach to an understanding of past societies and civilisations through their eating and drinking traditions, codes and systems of values.

This last-mentioned is my particular passion: what people choose to eat or refuse to eat, and why – from pig's blood and fish livers to cactus buds, stinging nettles, honeysuckle roots and anything else with edible potential. Through gastronomic history I begin to comprehend the interdependence of, and interrelationships between, cuisine and culture, agriculture and religion, the forces that shape and secure a society. I recognise the unbecoming isolationism of a good many food scientists, such as the biochemist of long standing who naively expressed his surprise, during a radio interview, that the Church could have an influence – and such an influence! – on diet and what people eat.

Gastronomy solves linguistic mysteries. At last I understand why *zuppa inglese* is so called, and how it fits into Italian culinary tradition. (It doesn't translate as English soup, as might be assumed. *Zuppa* originally meant bread soaked in wine, or other liquid – like the French '*souppes*', the English '*sops*'. A fifteenth-century Italian recipe for 'Suppa dorata' calls for pieces of bread dipped in beaten egg, with sugar and rosewater, fried in butter and served sprinkled with more sugar – something like French toast, as we call it, or *pain perdu* in France. So: *zuppa inglese*, with cake rather than bread, soaked in rum or wine, plus sweet custard, *crème anglaise* in French – it all falls into place.)

Let's go back to the fourth century BC, when Archestratus conceived gastronomy as the pleasure of taste pursued according to a gastronomic code or set of rules. According to third-century chronicler Athenaeus, Archestratus was 'impelled by love of pleasure, [and] diligently traversed all lands and seas in his desire . . . of testing carefully the delights of the belly'. Having achieved this, he faithfully recorded 'whatever and wherever there is anything best that is eatable or drinkable', and for his noble epic chose the title *Gastronomia* – literally, rules for the stomach, or what is best to eat where, when and how – anticipating by many centuries today's gastronomic tourist guides. If you go to Byzantium, he advised, 'get a slice of sword-fish, the joint cut right from the tail'. But the intention of Archestratus was less to regulate than to advise and counsel. He was wise enough to realise that rules and laws relate to actions, not objects, and his writings reflect his understanding that '*gastronomia*' meant recommendations relating to the nourishing of the individual, to eating and enjoyment.

Now let's skip to Renaissance Italy and the 'scheme for living' Platina outlined in his book *De Honesta Voluptate et Valitudine* – literally, Of Honest Indulgence and Good Health – which, incidentally, is credited as the first printed cookery book (dated approximately 1472). Many editions of Platina's book, translated into Italian, French, German, and possibly other European languages – but not English – circulated throughout Europe in the sixteenth and seventeenth centuries, its popularity probably as much due to its philosophy as its recipes, almost all of which were lifted, albeit with acknowledgment, from a contemporary Italian manuscript). In fact, the adoption of Italian culinary modes and manners by the French court owes as much to this book as to Catherine de Medici and her army of Italian cooks.

Like Archestratus, Platina gave advice on where, when and how best to eat particular foods as part of his 'scheme for living'. He explained:

I have written about the nature of things, and of meats, of health and a scheme for living, which the Greeks call diet, adding instructions for curing the sick. For indeed this little work and institution is proper and necessary to every citizen, according to the authority and teachings of the philosophers; as in olden times he who in times of war saved a citizen's life deserved much civic recognition, so now in time of peace he who saves others by giving a plan for living well would seem to merit the same. They may hold up food to me, as to a gluttonous and greedy man, as to one who panders the instruments of incontinence and other encouragements for the intemperate. Would that they were used to moderation and economy, as is Platina . . .

Or, as Brillat-Savarin wrote subsequently, 'a science which nourished men was at least as valuable as that which taught how to kill them'.

The motto for Platina's 'scheme for living' might well have been 'Enjoy in moderation', a message that even then probably fell on as many deaf ears as it does today. For several hundred years afterwards, 'schemes for living' revolved more around survival of the fittest, in a social sense. It was not until after the French Revolution – when

Australia was but a fledgling colony more intent on survival than on 'schemes for living' – that gastronomy reappeared in France, under the patronage of, in the first instance, Grimod de La Reynière, and subsequently, Brillat-Savarin, both of whom insisted on the primacy of the pleasures of the table.

Grimod de La Reynière is best remembered for his series of *Almanach des Gourmands*, which established him as the father of gastronomic journalism. Eight volumes were published between 1803 and 1812, with four separate editions of the first year. This first one was little more than a listing of produce, by month and by season, together with advice on how these ingredients could (should! dictated Grimod) be accommodated, and addresses of the best suppliers in Paris. The contemporary success and fame of the *Almanachs* was partly due to their content (they appealed to the nouveaux riches who needed to know where to shop-and-be-seen) but also rested on the style in which they were written – witty, amusing, allusive and often sardonic, com-posed with an acid-tipped pen.

Grimod romanticised markets, making them a temple of gour-mandism instead of mere centres of exchange. Markets brought to Paris (and so, in his estimation, to Civilisation and Culture) the prod-ucts of provincial Nature, and Grimod provided lyrical and greedily anticipatory descriptions of sleek cattle and gleaming fish, innocent lambs and barrels of golden butter, all offering themselves to the adoring palates of the city – and ready to receive the reverent minis-trations of the chef.

As Grimod de La Reynière might have envisaged it, gastronomy is the enjoyment of the very best in food and drink, an interpretation close to that of Archestratus but far removed from Brillat-Savarin's now classic definition. Curiously, Grimod's writings faded into near-obscurity while the work of Brillat-Savarin went through twenty editions in the fifty years after his death (a few months after the book's publication) and is still in print. Though Grimod offered readers the necessary information – where to shop, what to buy, how to prepare it – he forgot the underlying philosophy, the 'scheme for living'. Brillat-Savarin spent years refining his philosophy, eventually condensing it into the twenty aphorisms prefacing the series of 'gastronomic meditations' which constitute the *Physiology of Taste*. These have since been effectively enshrined as the gastronomic canon – maxims such as 'The Creator, who made man such that he must eat to live, incites him to live by means of appetite, and rewards him with pleasure'; 'Animals feed; man eats; only the man of intellect knows how to eat'; and 'To entertain a guest is to make yourself responsible for his happiness so long as he is beneath your roof'.

In the English-speaking world there was a similar upsurge of interest in gastronomy in the nineteenth century. In Australia it was a doctor, Philip Muskett, who proposed (and promoted) a 'scheme for living' for all those who made their home in the Antipodes, and entitled it *The Art of Living in Australia* (1893). Muskett's vision was bold and unmistakably gastronomic, and entailed no less than a complete reform of Australian eating habits – or, as he viewed them, expatriate and inappropriate Anglo-Saxon eating habits. He argued that lifestyle should accord with climate, and that applied to dress, housing, and, most importantly, diet and eating habits. An English style of eating (and cooking) was incompatible with Australia, which, at least in the southern temperate regions with which he was familiar, basked in a Mediterranean climate. Almost a century before it became fashionable, Muskett advocated for Australians a Mediterranean diet and style of eating that incorporated more fruit and vegetables than people habitually ate – and especially more salads – together with more fish and seafood, and less meat. His reasons for moderating Australians' extraordinarily high meat consumption had little to do with health (though Muskett, along with other medicos of his day, believed an excess caused gout and other illnesses) and a lot to do with enjoyment – the monotony of meat three times a day was hardly an incentive to mealtime pleasure.

When Archestratus and, in his footsteps, Grimod de La Reynière, established the relation between gastronomy and excellence, it was inevitable that gastronomy should be associated only with fine dining, as most dictionary definitions would have us believe, rather than reflective eating. It was almost as inevitable that the term should be corrupted, in an upwardly mobile sort of way, such that a plate of bread and cheese is often seen as incompatible with gastronomy. At the same time, the motto 'Enjoy in moderation' has been hijacked by the liquor industry as its slogan. If today you question the proverbial man in the street, the likely answer is that gastronomy represents fancy food and drink – especially when consumed at someone else's expense. This is wrong. If one had to find another shell for gastronomy's kernel, it would be 'reflective eating'.

Beneath the banner of gastronomy, eating implies the enjoyment of eating, the recognition of the balance between enjoyment and health. The key to life is a healthy appetite. '*Moi, j'ai toujours faim,*' (I'm always hungry) confided Robert Courtine, venerable French food writer and critic, then around 70. A healthy appetite implies a healthy joie de vivre. Healthy, meaning balanced, in proportion, neither too much nor too little, acknowledging limits and recognising that more, in terms of quantity, does not necessarily correspond to more, in terms of pleasure. Unhealthy appetites express themselves in perversions – as epitomised in the feast given by that uncouth upstart Trimalchio, in Petronius' *Satyricon*.

Healthy appetites are rewarded with pleasure. Eating means pursuing and celebrating flavour. It involves an understanding of physical environments, what they can produce and when each product is at its best. But eating is a convivial activity, and solitary pleasures are rarely so pleasurable as those shared. Both 'reflective eating' and 'schemes for living' need words to express them. Gastronomy without language is as unimaginable as a celebration without champagne, a pub without beer. Their relationship is as intimate and natural as that between wine and food, the one presaging and prolonging the pleasures of the other. As wine is to food, so is language to gastronomy. Brillat-Savarin was hardly the first to remark that the pleasures of the table include the charm of conversation. Language is a means of anticipating, prolonging, repeating, intensifying the gastronomic experience – and also an invitation to others to share it.

WRITING ABOUT FOOD

When there is no more cuisine in the world, there will be
no more literature, no quick and sparkling wit,
no friendly relationships; there will be no longer
be any social unity. — Antonin Carême

WHY DO I WRITE ABOUT FOOD? Because I enjoy it – food, and
writing about it. Other people write about politics, or fishing, or education; I write about food and cooking and eating, about food in
history and in society, about the meanings of food and how they enrich
our everyday lives.

What most people associate with food writing are the books and

•

•

articles firmly focused on the material substance, foods eaten (as in restaurant reviews) and to be eaten (as in recipes). But food is such a vast subject that writing about food can take many forms, from scientific and technical articles about agriculture and food production through food-and-travel stories to recipes and cookbooks and menus. As Jean-François Revel wrote, 'Every menu is an exercise in rhetoric'. Food writing can have – and perhaps ought have – an educational bent, aiming to increase the general understanding of all aspects of food and of different cultural traditions. It can raise the general level of public consciousness and at the same time acknowledge the efforts of individual producers and cooks. Above all, however, it should provide pleasurable reading.

Producing pleasurable reading usually comes more easily to those who themselves find pleasure in food, cooking and eating. As they like to share their pot so they share their enthusiasm, believing that food writers also have the happy duty of encouraging people to enjoy what they eat and to eat for pleasure rather than profit – profit in the form of protection against cancer, heart disease and potential allergies. Those who live in fear of these natural maladies are also, I suspect, those who never read food writing (statements of nutrient benefit on a packet of low-cholesterol mayonnaise are a class apart). Similarly, people who take pleasure in reading about food and enjoy food writing for its evocative, nostalgic, appetite-arousing appeal are also those who find honest delight in eating and drinking. In this latter group are good food writers – such as Elizabeth David and her compatriot Jane Grigson.

Elizabeth David saw the food writer as a counterpart to the theatre or music critic. As she wrote in *An Omelette and a Glass of*

Wine (1984), 'If a food writer does not exercise his or her critical faculties to a high degree and with a backing of informed experience, he or she is not doing his or her job'. Reacting against the 'idiotic convention' of cookery articles, Elizabeth David wrote on subjects as unconventional as eccentric books, a delicatessen exhibition and what she called 'a particularly awful restaurant', in a style that was individual and forthright. She did not hesitate to exercise her critical faculties, to praise or censure (describing a chicken and veal pie that even her cat would not eat), and her opinions were informed, discerning and balanced.

What Elizabeth David was implying in her statement, I think, is that a food writer should have the ability to taste, interpret those tastes, assess them and report the results in such a way the whole experience can be understood (vicariously experienced, even) by readers. The purpose of a restaurant review is not solely to pass judgment on a particular restaurant, in the form of stars or chef's toques or marks out of twenty, but also to pass on, to the reading public, information about that restaurant. Like any other critical review, it should judge and evaluate but at the same time should report and provide illustration and description in such a way that the reader can sense what is being described and form an independent opinion. Invariably, the food writer's judgment is nuanced by personal taste, but it also reflects the general palate, which universally finds fault in a dish that is burnt when it should be lightly toasted, lukewarm when it should be hot, mushy when it should be crisp. Like the singer's missed note, these are obvious flaws.

When the food writer silently asks: Are the raw materials good? Is the cooking good? Is the service satisfactory, the experience

•

•

enjoyable? the answers cannot be anything other than subjective judgments, but at the same time they bring into play previous experiences against which the present one is assessed. Somewhere I have a memory of the most delicious mango I have ever eaten (peeled, sliced and lightly chilled, in the restaurant of a Kuala Lumpur hotel), and likewise of the worst croissant I have ever had the misfortune to pay for, and whenever I eat a mango, or a croissant, I can compare and rate it against other mangoes, other croissants. My judgment is no less valid for being subjective; the accumulation of experiences provides a sound base. Just as writers on politics, fishing or education have the credentials to sustain their opinions and judgments, so the food writer typically has a reliable memory of foods eaten and evaluated.

Good food writing, like all good writing, must engage and retain the reader's interest. But writing about food, about eating food, is different from writing about politics or education. Engaging the reader's attention means communicating sensual responses and impressions, which means that the food writer has to find apposite words to translate them. There are many problems fitting slippery words to ephemeral foods and wines – and equally with the reverse operation, imagining foods and wines from the words written and spoken about them – but, usually, words are the only means we have. The correspondence might not be exact – going from foods to words to foods one never arrives back at the exact same starting point – but it can come close. And the translation of experience to language need not be literal; indeed, it is probably more evocative if not. In his poem 'Correspondances', Baudelaire – who in my imagination is forever parading his green lobster through the absinthe haze of Parisian cafés – envisaged a kind of harmony of the senses where '*les parfums, les*

•

•

couleurs et les sons se répondent' (perfumes, colours and sounds respond to one another), describing a fragrance as 'fresh as a young child, sweet as an oboe, green as a meadow'.

The wine writer faces the same task of communicating a taste experience by translating, via the intellect, the reactions of the senses. A phrase such as 'lean, classy, herbaceous with a hint of oak, well structured and elegant' gives you little idea of flavour, though it would reassure you of the wine's acceptability. If the wine were described as 'reminiscent of passionfruit and cats' piss' you probably wouldn't let it within cooee of your waiter's friend. The words 'smoky, gooseberry, passionfruit' almost let you see the wine and feel it splashing down your gullet. Or, if you can't taste it in your imagination, you might at least be inspired to want to taste it, which suggests that another purpose of talking about wine is to invite you to drink it, as writing about food invites you to eat. (In this respect an allusion to cats' piss is decidedly discouraging.)

The danger is that the descriptions, however concrete, can stray recklessly far from everyday experience and become ridiculously recherché with phrases such as 'like lime marmalade on freshly buttered wholemeal toast'. To avoid such flights of fancy would probably mean the development of a standard glossary, a list of words, each paired to a sensual impression, which could be learnt through wine appreciation classes just as in the old days you learnt by rote your weekly French vocab. There are obvious benefits in such a system, but it takes the fun out of reflecting and seeking the right words.

Wines can be described by likening them to fruits and other familiar foods but our lexicons for food, in comparison, are woefully inadequate, as Christopher Driver pointed out in his book *The British at Table, 1940–1980* (1983). He sees a partial explanation in the fact that wine is optional, complex and infinitely varied, while food is a necessity, and only occasionally is it necessary to draw attention to the finer points of discrimination. With its limited vocabulary, food writing can trivialise language, as in restaurant reviews where the same adjectives tend to appear over and over: creamy, succulent, tender, flavoursome, appetising. And the same superlatives: splendid, ambrosial, sublime. As the English humorist Miles Kingston advised, tongue firmly in cheek, 'When out good food guiding you should keep an eager eye open for the five great qualities in cooking: crispness, freshness, fluffiness, lusciousness and exquisiteness. The five bad things to avoid are: blandness, dryness, tiredness, tinnedness and leftoverness. The greatest quality of all is crispness without, meltingness within.' Like the characters in Ionesco's play, *The Bald Prima Donna*, who, father and mother, son and daughter, aunt and uncle, grandfather and cousin, were *all* called Bobby Watson, food words can, if overused, become so devalued as to lose significance.

Language probably serves us better when we are called upon to compare and discriminate rather than where we are required to translate sensual impressions in such a way that others can understand them. A French experiment recorded over 2000 different words employed by the 1368 members of tasting panels which evaluated 150 cheeses according to their appearance, taste and texture. Many of the words used had the same, or very similar, meanings – genuine, authentic, typical, true. Certain qualities of the cheeses attracted clusters of words, such as supple, creamy, melting, smooth, soft and homogeneous to describe the unctuosity of one group of cheeses.

•

•

When different people used the same adjectives to describe the taste of a cheese they were usually representing objective qualities – ammoniacal, buttery – but for vague descriptions such as classic, rustic, tempting and refined there was no consistent pattern of use, suggesting that words such as these are almost meaningless for representing the taste experience.

Christopher Driver believes words and phrases can only be useful in food criticism if descriptive and evocative, as opposed to approving or disapproving, which means eschewing words like 'delicious', 'luscious', 'stunning' and any other adjectives which simply say 'Yum, I enjoyed it'. 'Evocative' is, I think, the key word; the description should evoke an image, whether visual or otherwise – fish made into a poultice with the texture of an Irish bog, boeuf bourguignon with the texture of compressed string and the flavour of unploughed fields (to borrow two of Christopher Driver's examples). We might not know what unploughed fields taste like, but we can imagine (and the idea of unploughed fields is sufficiently imprecise – unlike that of cats' piss – to give rise to all sorts of associated images).

The naivety of children often allows them to make, more easily than artful adults, the imaginative, sensual-literalist leaps of language that magically and instantaneously transform a taste experience. Christopher Driver's four-year-old daughter reported that a salad of baby squid tasted of spiders; and my three-year-old son, waking up to a batch of cherry tartlets – I had used pale pink cherries which, on cooking, had become fleshily translucent – exclaimed with pleasure, 'Nipple tarts!' Baudelaire would, I'm sure, approve.

In instances such as this, when the food itself is firmly anchored in reality, and the ideas and images float around it in semi-detached balloons, a certain leeway is tolerated in the matching of words to tastes. When the words come first and the food is expected to match them, then lack of correspondence can be a problem. Some food descriptions are so far removed from the actuality they purport to describe as to be downright deceitful – especially on airline menus, where what you are given bears little relation to what you thought you'd receive. That 'barramundi' could have been anything white and flaky, the 'smoked chicken' could be tanned tofu.

The French philosopher Henri Bergson recognised how language, preceding, can affect sensual perceptions. 'The influence of language on sensation goes deeper than is generally believed,' he wrote. 'Not only does language make us believe that the sensations we experience are invariable, but it sometimes deceives us with respect to a sensation. Thus, when I eat a dish reputed to be exquisite, its name, expanded by the reputation of that dish, comes between my sensation and my consciousness. I can persuade myself that the taste pleases me, whereas a slight effort of attention would prove the contrary to me.'

Words can certainly influence the flavour of food – or at least, how we perceive it. A slice of delicious rare roast beef might suddenly turn nauseating the moment its purchase from the *boucherie chevaline* (horse meat butcher) is revealed, and *andouillette*s (tripe sausages) might be enjoyed only so long as their intestinal origins are denied. Under the name of *boeuf bourguignon* the humble stew might be savoured with more finesse.

Yet words are the food writer's tools, and their usage entails a certain responsibility; they should not be written carelessly. The exercising of critical faculties also means finding the right words. It involves a double translation – from taste buds to brain, from image to the language. In his book, *Anatomy of Criticism* (1957), Northrop Frye wrote that criticism exists because 'criticism can talk, and all the arts are dumb'. Writing about food is expressing the voice of food, and we, the food writers, are the mediators.

THE MEANING OF FOOD

There is a Vietnamese saying which roughly translates as 'A morsel of food is like a morsel of shame', for the offer of food can be as much an expression of contempt as of generosity.
— Annabel Doling

--- ---

'FOR WHAT IS FOOD?' queried Roland Barthes, immediately replying: 'It is not only a collection of products that can be used for statistical or nutritional studies. It is also, and at the same time, a system of communication, a body of images, a protocol of usages, situations, and behaviour.'

Tourists in Rome can go to St Peter's and make their confessions in any language – including Esperanto, the so-called universal language. Esperanto might hope to supply the words, but the universal medium of *communication* is food.

Words are still important, but food – in its widest sense, including drink – provides the inspiration. Everyone has opinions, experiences, memories of food, and all are equally valid; food is the democratising influence par excellence. At a dinner in France that threatened to be as boring as a university lecture on logic – the aperitif conversation consisted of an alphabetic recital of the various *départements* and the corresponding numbers on car registration plates – I introduced the topic of food, based on what we were eating and about to eat. Eventually it animated the whole table, and I heard the wartime recollections of a sprightly grandmother who, with sparkling eyes (accompanied by flashes of jealousy in those of her husband), told of the illicit chocolates she kept in a drawer with her illicit nylons, and how she rationed them – and how the rats discovered her treasure before she had managed to consume it all.

In the Languedoc village of Nizas (population: 391; attractions: medieval château, now a winery), I was introduced to the wild asparagus that grew under the disused railway line, the wild capers that were pickled in late spring, and the wild leeks that sprang up amongst the vines and opened the opportunities for communication. 'You've never eaten *poireaux sauvages*?' asked one of the tribe of black-suited old men who would pass by our house on their morning rounds. 'Don't you have wild leeks in Australia?' Early one morning one of the old men (we never reached the intimacy of introductions, so had to bestow our own names; this one we called *Poireau Sauvage*) brought a bundle of wild leeks and told me how they should be prepared. There was only one way, and that was to trim them, boil them until tender, dress with oil and vinegar, and eat them lukewarm as a first course. I did as instructed, and next day offered him a taste. That exchange initiated a kind of relationship. These village elders were fascinated by *les étrangers*, the foreigners, and came to learn as much about Australia as we did about Nizas. It was almost incomprehensible to them that there should be a country where wild leeks were not part of the landscape, where sheep looked after themselves without the constant care of a shepherd, where villages were 50 rather than five kilometres apart. We might as well have come from outer space as from the other side of the globe. Without that spark of a common interest in food, how much poorer would be my understanding of Nizas and its inhabitants!

People who are interested in food, and who care about what and how they eat and drink, are generous with it, and generous by nature. Travelling in Normandy, near Mayenne, I was given a lift by a farmer who incidentally asked whether I had ever drunk the local speciality, bottle-fermented cider, *cidre bouché*. To my negative, he wheeled round and stopped in front of a very ordinary-looking service station. 'She's never had *cidre bouché*,' he offered, by way of explanation; so we sat down and drank a bottle. By then, it was nearly *midi*, so he invited me to lunch at the farm. But first, we had to make a detour to a certain *épicerie* to buy another Normandy speciality, camembert – this particular one made by his mother-in-law. Dinner was roast leg of lamb with green beans, plus the cheeses, fruit and patisseries – all leftovers, I was told, of a First Communion feast of the day before. And so I learnt about the ritual of the First Communion, on the first Sunday in May, and its family significance, and the associated traditions of eating and drinking. I learnt about camembert and Normandy cows, and the grass that grows overnight, and the symbiosis of cows and apple trees. And I learnt that people who enjoy eating and drinking and talking with honest gusto are rarely inhibited or hypocritical or cheerless.

All food carries a meaning, whether through symbolic associations or through the way in which it is used to deliver a message. The ornamental sugar and marzipan sculptures of Renaissance banquets represented Love, or Peace, or the union of two powerful families. Different dishes, often richer and more elaborate than our everyday fare, are offered to welcome and honour guests. Green salads with an abundance of fresh herbs announce spring, and a pot of steaming soup in the centre of the table signifies generosity, an invitation to share. A golden soufflé can be an expression of love, an overdone chop a demonstration of disaffection. On learning that Matisse was staying to dinner, Gertrude Stein's cook, Hélène, who had taken a dislike to the artist, retorted: 'In that case I will not make an omelette but fry the eggs. It takes the same number of eggs and the same amount of butter but it shows less respect, and he will understand.' And of course, the refusal of food is the ultimate statement of distrust, rebellion or autonomy.

Symbolic significance can be individual or universal, or both. For me, puftaloons (fried scones) say Queensland, because it was always my father who cooked them then saturated them in golden syrup, while telling us about his Queensland boyhood, which included puftaloons. Sea urchins I associate with the Mediterranean, because the first one I ever ate was on a beach near Palermo. These personal meanings are subsumed into a larger scheme in which meat is associated with masculinity, roast meats carry a higher prestige than boiled or stewed, and any sort of bubbly wine intimates a celebration.

•

•

It is because food is nuanced at different levels that banquets can make statements, taking advantage of the symbolic attributes of particular foods – and the more complicated the message, the deeper the symbolism. Cookbook author Claudia Roden once described a wedding reception in Italy where an ornate, towering, multi-tiered wedding cake was wheeled into the salon for guests to admire and applaud – while in the kitchen behind, another, more ordinary cake was being cut up and packed into special little take-home boxes. Here, symbolism was all – the cake itself had been hired for the occasion, the *pasticceria* offering several models from which to choose. Similarly, the decorative pieces sculpted from ice or margarine – perhaps in form of a coat of arms, or a state emblem – are pure symbolism, having no edible function whatsoever. But artefacts such as these, however impressive, are only accessories; their message is limited. It is only when we take the food into our bodies and incorporate it, together with its values and meanings, that its meaning can be realised.

Gastronomy, said Brillat-Savarin, 'examines the effect of food on man's character, his imagination, his wit, his judgement, his courage, and his perceptions, whether he be awake or asleep, active or at rest.' He expressed the general idea more succinctly in the best-known of his aphorisms: *Dis-moi ce que tu manges, je te dirai ce que tu es* – Tell me what you eat, I will tell you what you are.

It's trite, and a generalisation, but has validity. It's a maxim that can be applied at many levels. Most simply, it says that nationalities or regionalities can be differentiated on the basis of national or regional diet or food preferences: I like cheese and milk chocolate, therefore I am Swiss; he eat lots of barbecued beef, he is Argentinian. At a deeper level, eating habits are identified with national character. Indeed, some

of the most clichéd images of a country are those which associate particular national characteristics with typical national foods. Australian
apathy in the late nineteenth century was blamed on a monotonous
diet of meat, bread and tea, as Francis Adams wrote in *The Australians:
A Social Sketch* (1893).

> *The horrible condition of the coatings of stomachs perpetually drenched
> with tannin (speciously termed 'tea') doubtless counts for something in
> the action and reaction of body and climate, climate and body.*
>
> *After a good spell of drought, endured on a diet of mutton, bread,
> jam, and stewed Bohea, one's indifference to life becomes all but
> complete.*
>
> *There is nothing wild or hysterical about it.*
>
> *It is merely a profound and passionless heedlessness of danger
> and death.*

Perhaps perceptions depended on the diet of the writer, for
Marcus Clarke, writing at about the same time, saw a meat-centred
diet producing slightly different characteristics in Australians. Meat-
eaters, he said, are 'rash, gloomy, given to violences'. In one of his
essays he even ventured a portrait of 'The Future Australian Race',
based on the Australian appetite for meat:

> *The custom of meat-eating will square the jaw and render the hair coarse
> but plentiful. The Australasian will be a square-headed, masterful man,
> with full temples, plenty of beard, a keen eye, a stern and yet sensual
> mouth. His teeth will be bad, and his lungs good. He will suffer from liver
> disease, and become prematurely bald; average duration of life in the
> unmarried, fifty-nine; in the married, sixty-five and a decimal.*

The conclusion of all this is, therefore, that in another hundred years the average Australasian will be a tall coarse, strong-jawed, greedy, pushing, talented man, excelling in swimming and horsemanship. His religion will be a form of Presbyterianism; his national policy a Democracy tempered by the rate of exchange. His wife will be a thin, narrow woman, very fond of dress and idleness, caring little for her children, but without sufficient brain power to sin with zest. In five hundred years — unless recruited from foreign nations — the breed will be wholly extinct; but in that five hundred years it will have changed the face of nature, and swallowed up all our contemporary civilisation.

Belief in the power of food to influence personality has waxed and waned. In the years immediately after the first world war, meat-eating was often linked to aggression and violence. The determining influence of food on character was a strong tenet of the Italian Futurist movement, spearheaded by Marinetti. In the *Manifesto of Futurist Cuisine* of 1930, Marinetti declared:

Though we recognise that in the past, men who have eaten badly or crudely have still been able to achieve great things, we proclaim this truth: one thinks one dreams one acts according to what one has drunk and what one has eaten.

Marinetti's passion was directed against pasta, which for centuries has been associated with Italians. In his view, pasta produced 'lassitude, pessimism, and a tendency to inactivity, nostalgia and neutralism', which conflicted with 'the mental vivacity and passionate, generous, intuitive soul of the Neapolitans'. Calling pasta 'an absurd Italian gastronomic religion', Marinetti campaigned for its abolition.

•

•

If there have been heroic fighters, inspired artists, orators capable of moving crowds, brilliant lawyers, determined farmers, it is in spite of the voluminous dishes of daily pasta. And it is because of eating it that they become sceptical, ironic and sentimental – characteristics which often constrain their enthusiasm.

The English writer Norman Douglas, who lived in Italy for many years, contributed an outsider's view. In *Old Calabria* (1915) he named envy as the Italians' most conspicuous native vice and attributed it to their meagre breakfast.

Out of envy they pine away and die; out of envy they kill one another. To produce a more placid race, to dilute envious thoughts and the acts to which they lead, is at bottom a question of nutrition. One would like to know for how much black brooding and for how many revengeful deeds that morning thimbleful of black coffee is responsible.

However reasonable Brillat-Savarin's saying appears, perhaps it would be wrong to take it too literally. It seems so natural that 'you are what you eat', in a figurative sense, that it is tempting to let the matter rest at the level of popular culture and folk wisdom, in the assumption that the relationship is one of simultaneity rather than one of causality. You can believe in its validity without pursuing the reasons why. Perhaps it works best as a literary device, allowing novelists to portray characters through what and how they eat and cook. Readers will recognise 'Mrs Jones' when they learn that she buys tinned peas and carrots, margarine and mincemeat, uses instant coffee and prepares it in a microwave. Mrs Williams can be nothing else but 'plump and jolly' after you read, in Marion Halligan's short story 'The Marble

•

•

Angel', that 'she cooked big roast dinners and steak-and-kidney puddings and light-as-air sponge cakes with strawberry jam and cream'.

It is tempting to leave it there, yet epidemiological studies show that butchers father more sons than daughters, a result interpreted as the result of a greater consumption of meat, and hence a greater supply of testosterone. Research indicates that different diets produce different body smells, that fragrances can modify mood, and that pheromones (present in certain wines and certain foods, such as truffles) can influence patterns of behaviour. So perhaps Norman Douglas and Francis Adams were hinting at a deeper reality when they associated caffeine and tannin with envy and pessimism – and perhaps Brillat-Savarin was exceptionally perceptive, not to say prophetic, when he invited our dietary confessions.

It all goes to show that food is far more than 'a collection of products that can be used for statistical or nutritional studies'. As our medium of expression as well as a way of reading others, it is undoubtedly a universal language.

FLAVOUR FIRST

The luscious, super-close, larger-than-life size photographs in recipe books say 'Admire me, eat me with your eyes,' not 'Cook me and offer me to your friends.'

--- ---

SOME YEARS AGO JEREMY RIFKIN, author of *Beyond Beef: The Rise and Fall of the Cattle Culture* (1992), ran a campaign to encourage Americans to reduce their beef consumption by half. He argued that regions in South America were being devastated to satisfy the American – and world – appetite for hamburgers and steaks. And for the same reason, a high proportion of the world's grain production was undergoing a secondary transformation before making its appearance as lean beef.

Rifkin had no quarrel with environmentally friendly, agriculturally sustainable beef, pure as innocence and natural as honesty (which – by and large, for better or worse – Australia eats). Nevertheless, his campaign has global relevance here: if we all eat less, any domestic surplus can be exported to America, which then won't compromise third world peasants, who then can (whether they want to or not) return to traditional subsistence, and the world will stay as we like it.

I would be happy to reduce my beef consumption by fifty per cent – indeed, I probably have already done so – but my motives are gastronomic, and I'd like the quid pro quo assurance of an improvement in quality. And by quality I refer principally to flavour. I'd be satisfied with half as much steak if it announced itself on the palate with a flavour that could be remembered. Tenderness to me is secondary, which is exactly the contrary of the way the values are seen to stand in society at large. Flavour-wise, and unless it's been aged by caring butchers, most steak is drab. Sure, it has maximal protein, minimal fat, just as the doctors ordered – and for them, flavour is not usually a priority.

Increasingly, it's the doctors' orders that dictate the way our foods are. We all know that animal products, sensitive souls that they are, have been feeling unloved and unappreciated since the discovery of cholesterol. So when the National Research Council of America was asked to look at new technologies and processes that could improve 'the nutritional attributes of animal products' (in other words, reduce fat and cholesterol contents), it had the Board on Agriculture come up with a few ideas. No probs, said the Board; we'll fix it, easy. And it

•

•

outlined its solutions in a report entitled *Designing Foods: Animal Product Options in the Marketplace* (1988).

The easiest fix is making sure the animal grows proportionately more protein and less fat. To do this, you control what the animal eats, and how much, and when, and at the same time you make sure that what does get eaten is preferentially transformed into protein by means of anabolic (hormone) implants, from birth to judgment day. (Anabolic estrogenic implants are described as 'effective repartitioning agents that modify growth by shifting nutrients from fat to protein accretion'. These implants, also known as hormone growth pro-motants, are licensed for use in cattle in Australia but are rarely used, principally because Australian beef is predominantly pasture-fed but also because European regulations prohibit the entry of meat from animals which have been treated with such implants.)

Fixing chickens so that they don't come with flabs of fat is also easy, said the Board. First, choose your genetically programmed chickens; next, feed the them the right feed – and don't forget to add the feather meal for the last couple of weeks.

Now, manipulating the animals like so many cogs in a machine is bad enough, but there's something nauseating and cannibalistic about feeding the poor birds with the remnants of their forbears. In the industry it's called – with a hint of irony? – 'recycling'; and in inten-sive animal production, there's an awful lot of recycling, including feeding mashed up and pelleted sheep heads to English cattle. If that's what producers have to do in order to offer us what we are told we should be eating, I'd rather wiggle my toes in the sand for pipis.

Why is it that we, as consumers, should be so patronised, told what's good for us? Why, at the same time, are our foods manipulated

•

•

to bring them closer to someone else's vision of what we ought be eating? 'Designing' foods – which has nothing to do with artful inter-pretations on large white plates nor with allegorical cornucopia – sounds chillingly brave-new-worldish. Its purpose likewise: to make it easier for us to do the right thing, mould us into acquiescence, take away temptations. Control us, straitjacket us, remove our choices – just as happens to the computer-managed animals.

I like to think that my life is what I make of it, and that I'm happy to accept the quota of years that is my due. Immortality, or even a couple more years, is not my goal. I don't want other people making decisions for me about what I should eat, and how I should live. Those remain my choice, and I have my own preferences and priorities and reasons for them.

So I find it easy to refuse lukewarm, nutritionally programmed beef and lacklustre chicken, however virtuous they are claimed to be, and live on lamb and fish (they haven't done anything to these, yet). I'd be happy to reduce my beef consumption by half if the beef I ate could be more flavoursome and more beefily individual, even if I had to pay twice as much for it. Being non-designed, non-industrialised, it prob-ably would cost more, but doesn't proper beef deserve luxury status? Remember, chicken was a luxury before the efficiency of the broiler industry reduced it to mediocrity. Eat less and enjoy it more – surely this is a cheaper, easier and potentially more popular solution than all the technology the National Research Council can come up with. Preferring flavour is at least as valid a justification for cutting beef consumption by half as the ruin of rainforests and the plight of the peasants in South America.

Such developments that pass for progress in the food industry have led a friend of mine to develop his theory of the convenience trade-off: whatever you gain in convenience you lose in quality and flavour. Whether packet hollandaise or instant polenta, dehydrated potato flakes or pre-grated parmesan or individual chicken breasts (yes, all that water used in processing washes away any flavour the poor bird may have originally had), time is sacrificed for flavour. He sees his theory epitomised in the fast-food industry, hamburger chains in particular. Not that he has anything against hamburgers; indeed, Robert Carrier's Beefburgers, included among his *Great Dishes of the World* and made with good-quality minced beef enriched with beef marrow, are perfectly respectable and properly delicious.

What upsets him more is that most consumers aren't even aware of the trade-off. Amazingly few people seem to care, or even realise, that eating could be better, more enjoyable, and those of us who do begin to question our own judgment. Is it really worth the time and effort, the dirt under the fingernails, for a month of authentically vine-ripened tomatoes? We all make compromises somewhere; I don't have hens to eat the weeds and vegetable scraps and supply me with beautiful fresh eggs though I know full well that genuinely fresh, free-range eggs are a superior product. But when people aren't even aware that there's an alternative to the weekly or fortnightly supermarket safari, that food is more than substances to keep us alive, then I start to have reservations about the future of the human race – as Marinetti questioned the future of Italy, in his opinion dragged low by the sheer mass of its habitual pasta.

Even though Australian foods are cheap by English and European standards, this cheapness is seen as not merely good fortune but also a virtue, and for food producers and retailers the raison d'être of their enterprise. Cheapness, convenience, standardisation: these are the qualities agribusiness thrives on and supermarkets trade on. Economies of scale and mechanisation are their buzz words. Foods become simply commodities to be bought and sold, transformed and transported in boxes with bar codes on the side. But as with convenience, cheapness and standardisation have their trade-offs in terms of flavour.

In Australia, agriculture is, and always has been, dominated by economics and get-rich-quick bonanzas; dollars and cents are the measure of its being. Agricultural policy – so far as there is one, and so far as I am aware – says nothing whatsoever about feeding and clothing the people of Australia, but an awful lot about exporting and developing new overseas markets for the purpose of making money. Other countries export an agricultural surplus; here exporting is agriculture's prime justification.

The story of Australian agriculture over nearly 200 years is one of making money by selling produce overseas. Without the English market the wool industry would never have got off the ground. Mutton was a by-product – merely 'the soil on which wool is grown', wrote Godfrey Charles Mundy in 1862. At the turn of the century the expansion of the dairy industry was a direct consequence of the development of refrigerated transport, which made it possible to sell butter and cheese to England; ditto the creation of the fat lamb industry. So the dairy industry made English-style butter and English-style cheeses; the fat lamb industry produced meat in accordance with English standards. For years, meat for export was quality-graded but meat for local consumption was not. (It's ironic that, not so long ago, one division of the CSIRO was researching ways and means of getting more fat into beef destined for the Japanese market, while another division was championing the-leaner-the-better!) Today's careful nurturing of the clean, green image of Australian produce is not primarily for the benefit of Australians but for consumers in overseas markets.

As cities expand, what used to be poultry farms, orchards, dairy farms and market gardens become merely real estate opportunities, and the resources that once produced food now yield profit only in terms of hard cash. The links between foods and their origins are being destroyed. So far removed are we from the primary source of our foods that we are conditioned to eat images, oblivious to the aroma, flavour or texture of the real thing.The luscious, super-close, larger-than-life size photographs in recipe books say 'Admire me, eat me with your eyes,' not 'Cook me and offer me to your friends.' In the mornings, only half awake, senses numbed, we crunch the picture on the packet of breakfast cereal at the same time as we use the words to crank our sluggish brains.

Our souls can respond to demonstrations of permaculture paradises, wastelands transformed into lush, fecund gardens where we have only to stretch an arm to touch perfection in the form of an odoriferous mango or, even more rare, the tasty tomato – but how many of us attempt to realise such a vision? Thus the consequence – a diversion of the senses, resort to memory. Memories are a wonderful resource, and better than MSG for adding flavour. Most adults can tell nostalgia-inspired stories about voluptuous crimson peaches, fresh from the tree, and creamy milk, straight from the cow. We're sophisti-cated enough to recognise that memories are as deceitful as a lover, but also astute enough to realise that today something is missing. More often than not, that something is flavour.

If small nations such as Norway and England can justify (and make succeed) policies for a greater measure of food self-sufficiency, then so should we, in Australia, in relation to regional areas. We should be making every effort to preserve or re-establish systems of agriculture that contribute directly to a region's food supply, identity and culture. In particular, we should encourage those systems which allow direct contact between producer and consumer. A measure of local self-sufficiency should encourage the realisation that buying food – 'provisioning' – is not just a matter of the greatest quantity for the least cost, and that flavour, freshness and authenticity are also part of the equation. Individuals can transform backyards, but the real challenge is to transform public values, to reduce our alienation from the sources of our foods so that we begin to eat, once again, real foods instead of images.

VEGS AND MEAT

Given the magazine's suggestions of what to eat in place of
meat — lentils in white sauce, walnut roast (basically walnuts,
breadcrumbs and rice), and curried nutmeat (tinned) — this lapse
of interest is hardly surprising. Indeed, for most of
vegetarianism's existence in Australia, its recipes have
represented a triumph of reason over pleasure.

TO START, LET ME SET DOWN my credentials. I am not a vegetarian. I respect vegetarian beliefs while not necessarily sharing them.
To vegetarianism in theory and to vegetarians in general I am sympathetic. I'm very fond of vegetables, but I also like meat – and fish, and

poultry, and game. I'm fond of animals, too, and I'm not convinced that by blackballing them I'd be doing myself, and the world in general, a favour. While I balk at eating dog, I guess I've managed to abstract myself from natural shudders as rabbits are clobbered inside sugar bags and sheep have their throats and then their bellies slit while hanging ignominiously by two shanks. I still eat and enjoy my roast free-range chicken and lamb fillets with quinces.

The gastronomic philosophy pronounced by Brillat-Savarin would seem to espouse eating anything that is potentially edible. 'The Creator, who made man such that he must eat to live, incites him to eat by means of appetite, and rewards him with pleasure.' Nowhere does this suggest that the domain of our taste preferences should be bounded by a dingo-proof fence, nor that to refuse the potential plea-sure of eating pork sausages or roast lamb is morally strengthening. I don't subscribe to the belief that all other species are at the mercy of man, but I recognise that eating is essential to survival. Like novelist Italo Calvino's Mr Palomar, I share in the 'man-beef symbiosis [which] has, over the centuries, achieved an equilibrium . . . and has guaran-teed the flourishing of what is called human civilisation'. I understand Mr Palomar's mood as he stands in line in the butcher's shop:

> *at once of restrained joy and of fear, desire and respect, egotistic*
> *concern and universal compassion, the mood that perhaps others express*
> *in fear . . . Though he recognises in the strung-up carcase of the beef the*
> *person of a disemboweled brother, and in the slash of the loin chop the*
> *wound that mutilates his own flesh, he knows that he is a carnivore,*
> *conditioned by his alimentary background to perceive in a butcher's shop*
> *the premise of gustatory happiness, to imagine, observing these reddish*

•

•

slices, the stripes that the flame will leave on the grilled steaks and the pleasure of the tooth in severing the browned fibre.

To be vegetarian is an individual choice. We all draw the line somewhere, marking off edible from inedible. For some it might only be insects – larvae, grasshoppers, cicadas – that fall below the line; others admit above it only vegetable products: fruits and vegetables, grains and seeds. To be able to choose how one eats is a luxury not available to those impelled by hunger or with barely enough to survive, nor to those captive of religious convictions and obliged to conform to the edicts of their faith. And today when vegetarianism is consciously chosen, it is usually for one or more of four simple motives: ethical, environmental, health or economic.

At one period during our stay in France we feasted on a near-vegetarian diet – for economic reasons. A few minor glitches had interfered with the expected automatic transfer of funds and we were obliged to shrink our spending. I'd been reasonably frugal (except when it came to cheese) but for a few weeks there I had to be super-thrifty, and decided that the most expendable component of the budget was meat. It was fortuitous that soon after we moved into the first floor of Madame's house in Provence, near Carpentras, I had stocked the pantry with wine, oil, rice, pasta, chick peas, lentils and beans – the small white beans the French call *haricots de Soissons.* Madame's spring garden provided us with broad beans, there was fennel growing by the sides of the roads and wild leeks in the vineyards (though I decided against using these, since the vines had just been sprayed with copper sulphate).

On the other side of the village I could buy fresh eggs, from real,

•

•

dirt-scratching hens, and at the Carpentras market vegetables were almost absurdly cheap, especially the small tomatoes newly in season. The charcutier's pâté was relatively inexpensive, so it was still bread and pâté for lunch. On these rations we ate extraordinarily well, and some of the necessary inventions have remained amongst my favourite dishes – such as a ratatouille-like mixture minus the aubergines (which weren't quite in season at that time), in which I make an indentation with the back of a large spoon and drop in an egg to softly poach. We ate risotto, and pasta with tomatoes; we ate lentils in salad and with rice, in the Lebanese manner; we ate *bouillabaisse d'épinards*, using the roadside fennel; fresh broad beans with tomato sauce; and lots of bread. Our diet was virtually meatless and wonderfully diverse.

In similar financial circumstances about six months later I developed a new respect for potatoes, of which there was then a glut following the shortage and consequent high prices of the previous season. For a bag of 50 kilos I paid five francs, around one dollar. Not being Irish, I was obliged to be inventive, to produce as much magic as possible out of this brown sack in a wheelbarrow in the darkest part of the cellar, where the potatoes duly sprouted hairs and whiskers and did all they could to awaken my latent horror of red-backs and funnel-webs. I worked as much magic as I could with fifty cents worth of salted or smoked belly pork from the local charcuterie, or with chestnuts and brussels sprouts (the local vegetable – by this time we were in the north of France). I used them in thick, creamy soups with watercress which, unlike me, loved that damp, dank climate; in a crusty gratin, with the best *comté* cheese; and in Spanish omelettes, using farm-fresh eggs (delivered to the charcuterie every Tuesday and Friday). By Easter, when the sun occasionally showed itself and the monthly deliveries of heating oil could cease, we had demolished about two-thirds of the 50 kilos. One night we guiltily unloaded the remaining potatoes into a vacant ditch, where they became food for the hedgehogs.

Vegetarianism is, to say the least, topical. Health propaganda presents vegetables and fruits as far more important components of the diet than red-blooded meat, subtly demoting the latter to also-ran. Indeed, vegetarianism has almost attained gastronomic respectability; most restaurants naturally include vegetarian selections on their menus and some vegetarian restaurants achieve top-ranking status. This restores a balance that for too long has been over-weighted by meat – though there are good reasons why special-occasion restaurants should highlight meat, while at the local pasta palace meat dishes are exceptional. But to over-correct, to tilt it too far in that direction – by labelling meat 'unhealthy', for example – is to display an equally inappropriate chauvinism.

Food arouses passions, and what we choose to eat or not eat often represents passionately held personal ideologies. This tends to preclude any objectively reasoned debate. And issues become clouded when the argument takes place within a black-and-white frame that permits no shades. In the typical dichotomy the choice is between 'no meat' (or any other animal foods) and 'meat', as if these were the only possible choices available to us – when in fact most humans are omnivores. It depends on how far back down the evolutionary ladder you want to go, but there is clear evidence that chimpanzees, the species most closely related to primitive man, enjoyed animal snacks (insects, rodents and small mammals) and even preferred them to their basic diet of fruits, nuts, leaves and other plant products. According to anthropologist Richard Leakey, significant meat-eating was one of the characteristics that differentiated early *Homo* from his predecessors.

The evolutionary argument holds that vegetarianism is somehow more 'natural', based on the belief that primitive man was essentially vegetarian. But our cave-dwelling ancestors also enjoyed their taste of meat. In his history of vegetarianism, *The Heretic's Feast* (1993) Colin Spencer reports that 'hunting provided only a relatively small proportion of a tribe's food' (the proportion, he implies, being around 20 per cent). Perhaps 20 per cent *is* only a small proportion, but the proportion of animal foods in average Australian diets today is hardly different. According to the 1983 dietary survey in Australia, meat, meat products and fish accounted for 17 per cent of the total mass of foods (excluding tea, coffee, milk and other drinks) consumed by the average female, and 22 per cent for males. In terms of their contribution to the energy value of the diet (excluding energy contributed by alcoholic and non-alcoholic beverages), animal foods were far less important than the foods from the vegetable kingdom – cereals, fruits and vegetables, nuts and seeds – which together supplied nearly half the energy, compared with only 21 per cent from meats. (Most of the remainder came from milk and milk products, eggs, fats, sugar, snack foods and confectionery.)

Emotional appeals based on the assumed 'naturalness' of a vegetarian lifestyle are somewhat irrelevant today. Current debate on vegetarianism must start with the fact that, almost always, it is a conscious choice – a luxury that early hominids might not have enjoyed. Or rather, it is a conscious choice in the secular societies of the western world, and of the English-speaking world in particular, where food choices are markers of individuality and where vegetarianism is not part of a common background culture as it is in India, for example, nor of a dominant religion. When it is adopted as a deliberate choice, vegetarianism (or the rejection of meat) is usually justified by arguments that are sane, logical, credible and persuasive. I'm not convinced, however, that a total rejection of meat and other animal products is necessarily the only solution.

Food choices are an outward expression of the beliefs and values that shape an individual's lifestyle. Vegetarianism is thus a natural complement to a belief in the rights of animals or in the importance of preserving the environment. These are honourable concerns. But while abstinence from meat by motivated individuals might mean fewer animals slaughtered and less environmental destruction, the rights of animals (to enjoy living) might be better served by a more humane treatment during their life and at the abattoirs. Surely intensive animal production which treats animals as mechanical feed converters – battery chicken is one example – is less humane, less respectful of the animals, than allowing sheep and cattle to graze and grow fat on natural pastures. Yet would-be vegetarians tend to give up red meat before white.

As for preservation of the environment, in Australia kangaroos are an alternative to cloven-hoofed destroyers of native grassland. Arguments about the relative economics of meat and grain production are inappropriate and misdirected. While it might make sense in America to argue that one acre under wheat, or soybeans, or some other vegetable crop, would feed more people than that same acre devoted to meat production, here most of our meat is produced under conditions where crop farming is simply not an alternative. This is not to deny the environmental 'cost' of grazing – and overgrazing; but it is sheer obstinacy to ignore that otherwise unusable natural pastures can be converted into food for human consumption by animals, native or not. In parts of outback Australia prescribed stocking rates – two head of cattle per square kilometre, for example – are calculated within the limits of sustainability.

Grain production can be even more environmentally disastrous than raising of livestock. Each kilogram of bread we consume costs seven kilograms of irreplaceable soil, according to Tim Flannery in his book, *The Future Eaters* (1994). Further, grazing animals on pasture is probably less wasteful of non-replaceable energy sources; pasture beef production takes 30 calories of energy to yield 50 food calories while intensive grain production takes 40 calories of energy and intensive horticulture (northern hemisphere glasshouses) requires 5000 energy calories for 50 food calories.

Economic arguments for vegetarianism hold good when meat is a comparative luxury – which is not always the case in Australia where the less reputable portions (such as liver) might cost less than the broccoli that accompanies them. Health arguments carry more weight, though the concept of ranking diets in terms of 'healthiness' is about as relevant as a search for the most effective slimming diet. As far as I know, all the studies to date have compared groups of vegetarians with matched groups of people eating average amounts of meat, and there has been no research comparing the health benefits of a totally vegetarian diet with one that includes small amounts of meat and animal foods – red meats two or three times a month, say, as advocated in the Harvard model of the Mediterranean diet. There are entire communities living almost meatless lives – on isolated Greek islands, for example – whose citizens easily achieve the three-score-plus-ten despite a healthy intake of nicotine. Their diet, however, is determined

•

•

more than it is chosen, and I'm not sure that longevity per se is a meritorious goal.

Individual objections to eating meat can be justified by aesthetic repulsion – the sight of blood, the idea of eating flesh (which can carry intimations of cannibalism or of eating one's own mother). There are people, too, who honestly prefer the taste of vegetables and in refusing meat are simply following natural inclinations – though it's just possible that these preferences are culturally and ideologically influenced. Fifty years ago, there were some whose 'natural inclinations' were for people of the same sex, but whose inclinations were not expressed because they were culturally unacceptable. Today they are, because it is – and vegetarianism could be a similar story. A preference for vegetables might also be motivated by the images associated with them, one of the most potent of which, in this New Age, has been 'health', in whatever shape and form it is conceived.

From my non-vegetarian perspective I see the other side to the pro-vegetarian arguments. There are reason and valid evidence on both sides, and even the sanest Solomon would have difficulty granting one side more 'right' than the other. Believing is what matters. What and how one eats depends on individual convictions, and no amount of persuasion from the opposing side will change this. People have consciously chosen vegetarianism at least since the sixth century BC when the Pythagoreans, renouncing meat because it was linked to the sacrificial slaughter of animals to the Gods, reverted to the more primitive wild plants that, in some earlier era, might have been 'the food of the Gods'. Paradoxically, they also avoided the highly nutritious broad bean since the broad bean plant, having a hollow stem, was assumed to be directly linked to the Underworld. What the plant took from

•

•

there was directly passed to the bean, so that eating a broad bean was tantamount to eating a soul, or cannibalism. (Others have since argued that renouncing broad beans was a way of avoiding potential illness, since a small proportion of Mediterranean peoples have a genetic abnormality that interferes with their ability to digest broad beans.)

Historically, the forces of vegetarianism have waxed and waned. The word itself is not much more than a century old – previously, people who refused meat called themselves fruitarians. The movement was relatively strong, especially in Anglo and predominantly Protestant countries, in the second half of the nineteenth century, and the New South Wales Vegetarian Society was established in 1891. It seems to have faded around the 1920s, until another burst of interest saw the Australian Vegetarian Society formed in 1948. This enthusiasm again seems to have been ephemeral, since the Society's journal apparently ceased publication in the 1950s. Given the magazine's suggestions of what to eat in place of meat – lentils in white sauce, walnut roast (basically walnuts, breadcrumbs and rice), and curried nutmeat (tinned) – this lapse of interest is hardly surprising. Indeed, for most of vegetarianism's existence in Australia, its recipes have represented a triumph of reason over pleasure.

In its early heyday, vegetarianism was touted as being more healthy and more humane – just as it is today. However, more fire seemed to be reserved for the argument that meat had a stimulating effect and was therefore to be avoided – as though it were a magic mushroom that could make decent citizens lose all control. 'Flesh foods being more stimulating than nourishing, inflame the lower desires and passions,' wrote the Food Reform League in 1913. Meat was a poison, a cause of cancer; it encouraged intemperance, evoked cruelty, incited wars. All in all, meat was considered a thorough baddie. Such values can be difficult to discard.

Today's vegetarianism sometimes still represents meat as a nasty, as if to encourage feelings of repulsion. Becoming a member of the Australian Vegetarian Society is like taking the pledge. Members must swear that they have abstained from eating the flesh of animals for three months or longer.

Unfortunately, the legacy of the lunatic fringe still hangs over vegetarianism. Vegetarians are often singled out and expected to justify themselves and their choice of diet when others with non-mainstream food preferences are not. If I refuse a ham-and-mustard sandwich and am asked why, I can give any one of a number of explanations: I'm not hungry; I don't like mustard; I've given up ham for Lent; I'm on a low-salt diet; I have an allergy to wheat products; my religion forbids me to eat pork. All of these would be perfectly acceptable and would be sympathetically received. On the other hand, if I replied, 'I'm a vegetarian and I don't eat animal products', I suspect the response would be different. Not only do past images and popular perceptions (holier-than-thou zealots who measure out their lives in kidney beans) come into play, but vegetarians, consciously or not, set themselves apart from the mainstream by their non-conformity to prevailing mores, just as did Pythagoras all those centuries ago. (There are also those who use the unchallengeably high-minded principles of vegetarianism as a pretext for attempts to lose weight and a cover-up for anorexia).

The solution to the concerns motivating vegetarians is not necessarily a denial of meat. People could simply eat less of it. There are valid historic reasons for the status of meat, and dethroning meat in western culture would be difficult. But we could take a couple of steps backward and return to a more respectful appreciation of meat, as in the times when it had religious and sacrificial associations. This implies also encouraging a different approach towards slaughtering, and the development of less stressful slaughterhouse environments and possibly different systems of killing and butchering. Those who have eaten meat from farm-reared, humanely slaughtered animals remark on its flavour and tenderness. There are also valid historic reasons for the lowly ranking of vegetables (anyone could grow a few vegetables, but only the wealthy owned livestock). But the status of vegetables is changing, and could be raised even further if restaurants and cafés featured more vegetable (which is not necessarily to say vegetarian) dishes, especially as a first course, and more dishes in which vegetables were a necessary and substantial part of the dish.

I would like to think that there is a way of eating that reconciles many of the concerns motivating vegetarians – humanitarian, ecological and health – yet does not totally exclude meat and other animal products. That it is possible to develop a philosophy that respects these concerns and rejects the extreme of asceticism in favour of a healthy sensuality. And that in an environment of mutual respect there would be more tolerance of others whose eating habits are not our own.

PROFESSOR LUCULLUS IN THE

TWENTY-SECOND CENTURY

Material luxury that is not democratised will not survive . . .
the luxuries of the rich become the necessities of the poor.
Consider, for instance, white bread, bananas, and bathrooms.
— Olga Hartley and Mrs Leyel

IN THE TWENTIETH CENTURY, the world turned vegetarian. We're almost at the end of it, and it hasn't, but this was the prediction of Olga Hartley and Mrs Leyel in their pamphlet *Lucullus: The Food of the Future*, written a couple of years after publication of their best-known

•

•

collaboration *The Gentle Art of Cookery* (1925). Or rather, it was not so much a prediction as an hypothesis, the recollection of the fictional Professor Lucullus from an imagined vantage point in the twenty-first century.

It's a charming little book, whimsical and gently ironic. Nevertheless, the intent of the two authors was not just to entertain but rather to draw attention, in the post-war, pre-Depression era, to the very serious subject of feeding the world. Their visions of the society and food of the twenty-first century were based on a thorough study of contemporary trends in food production and trade, food preparation and consumption.

Seventy-odd years later, some of their predictions ring uncannily true. The first is that the civilisation of the future will be democratic: 'Material luxury that is not democratised will not survive . . . the luxuries of the rich become the necessities of the poor. Consider, for instance, white bread, bananas, and bathrooms.' Their second assumption is that people will predominantly live in cities, and all their food requirements would have to be imported. It follows from this, they reasoned, that the values of the city-dwellers would come to dominate the rest of the world. Anticipating an imbalance developing between urban and agricultural populations as civilisation becomes 'merely urbanisation', the two ladies suggested that the adequacy of food supplies would, in the future, depend less on nature than on economic and political forces. Nevertheless, they believed that artificial or imitation foods, though feasible, would be neither acceptable nor assimilable. Finally, they hypothesised that there would be almost universal acceptance of a mechanistic view of life, the body-as-machine to be fuelled and maintained.

•

•

These premises sustain the authors' representation of the late twentieth century through the backward-looking eyes of one Professor Lucullus, sometime in the twenty-first century. Their vision shows a civilisation dominated by Vegetarians ('apparently one of the many curious religious sects that flourished about that time') who, through campaigning in schools and lobbying of parliamentarians to pass a law prohibiting the consumption of animal food, succeeded in imposing their beliefs on the highly organised and centralised society of the time. With animals gone, this hypothetical society was reduced to imitation fibres for clothing and warmth. Fortunately, the scientists of the time had learnt a few PR tricks and were able to persuade the people that the artificial fabrics they had invented were good for their health.

Now, among the Vegetarians arose a fundamentalist sect of Neo-Vegetarians whose motto was 'The minority is always right'. They insisted that it was cruel to 'massacre' vegetables for harvest and that the only permissible food was ripe fruit which fell from the tree of its own accord. While this might have been admirable in terms of their beliefs, it was hardly a viable theory on which to sustain a population. So the Neo-Vegetarians turned to the scientists who, in this future era, were allowed to carry out whatever experiments they wished, regardless of possible results. The scientists, in response to this urgent request, created an alternative diet compounded of cellulose, alcohol, bacteria and tin. If nothing else, these scientists were wonderfully versatile, and all went well – until one species of bacteria was induced to feed upon steel. The results were disastrous: pipes, steel frames, railway lines all disappeared. The Neo-Vegetarians, one imagines, hid behind the dust as they fled.

The kidnapping of Glasgow by Mars brought the world to its senses and signalled the start of a reformation in which scientists, duly disciplined, would concentrate their research on a few essentials. Thus in the twenty-first century of Professor Lucullus, the power of the tides is used to allow three harvests a year, a greater proportion of the available plant and animal resources is cultivated or raised for food, and the balance of the environment is closely watched. The one failing of this idealised society, according to Professor Lucullus – or perhaps according to Miss Hartley and Mrs Leyel – is gluttony, with too much honour being paid to Professors of the Culinary Art. 'Our remote ancestors, who left cooking to the uneducated, must have been a hardy spartan race, and it is a pity we cannot emulate their simple unsophisticated virtues.'

Much has changed since the book's publication and many of its prophecies – including a dinner in 1989 of laboratory-bred bacteria, rubber, chalk, coal and clay – were plainly absurd. But a great deal is still relevant. Olga Hartley and Mrs Leyel were seriously concerned by the imbalance between agriculture and manufacture: 'Our democratic, highly organised industrial population, which either cannot or will not, or at any rate does not produce food, merely agglomerates and distributes it, is living in a hygienically drained, steam-heated, electric-lighted mansion, with a wolf in the basement.' Further, they were sensible enough to realise that, even then, 'Back to the land' was not a solution. 'Earnest philanthropists and politicians continually urge the population to spread out, or beseech municipal authorities to spread the population out, and it is being done more or less. Suburbs and dormitory towns are being spread out like jam on bread; rows of little villas, pavements, and concrete roads replace fields and lanes, farms and market gardens, but the process doesn't produce more food. If the inhabitants of the little houses have room in their gardens for more than the baby's perambulator and the dustbin, they grow geraniums and a calceolaria.' Motivated by the primacy of food production, what Olga Hartley and Mrs Leyel would probably have liked to see were more *productive* gardens; they did not like to see resources wasted. They would have approved of city greening programs that include 'edible ornamentals' – that is, plants that are both attractive and useful: citrus and almond trees in place of oleanders, beds of perennial herbs instead of annual flowers, windbreaks of olives, hedges of rosemary, street plantings of native plants with edible possibilities.

The dire predictions of Miss Hartley and Mrs Leyel have not (yet!) come to pass, but it is disturbing to realise that they are not entirely in the realm of fantasy. The same concerns which inspired their book are still present – concentration of population in the cities, alienation from the sources of food, agriculture and food production ruled by politics and economics. Let's time-transport Professor Lucullus to some time in the twenty-second century and listen to his reflections on the era he has lived through.

The Arcadian Eunomists have invited the eminent Professor Lucullus to address their end-of-year meeting. Now Professor Lucullus is a wise old soul who has not only survived the twenty-first century but is still in the prime of a long and useful life. Some of the members, it must be admitted, are hoping for a few clues to his longevity, believing that the longer they live, the more pleasures they can accumulate. The Professor, however, refuses to divulge his secrets, preferring to recall the formative years of his youth. 'Environmental pragmatism was the password of the time,' he began, 'and nowhere was it more evident than in the domain of food production.'

'People were concerned to make the most of natural resources, because even with the one-child policy population was still growing. Anything – leaves, weeds, algae – that transformed the sun's energy into organic compounds was a potential food. The cost of double conversion was prohibitive, and so the grazing of livestock was gradually phased out; also, sheep and cattle wasted a good proportion of the plant food available to them by trampling on it. So animal foods were eliminated from the diet – except milk; people balked at calcium-enriched wattle-seed extract. Instead, huge automated dairies were set up outside the gigapolis for the express purpose of producing milk from highly efficient cloned cows that were fed enzyme-activated, pre-digested rations to obviate the wasteful loss of energy through cud-chewing. For ease of transport, all the milk was dehydrated at the factory and the water returned to the cows. In the gigapolis, central depots reconstituted the milk, sterilised it and delivered it to households every month, on a roster basis – you see how efficient their planning was?

'All foods were home-delivered. A long time ago, well before this, people used to go out every few days, or weekly, to select and buy the goods they needed from a variety of suppliers, then transport them back home. Obviously this was inefficient and economically wasteful, so the government set up a network of Distribarns that delivered everyone's orders monthly. We don't know who invented the Compubuy system, but it revolutionised shopping. It took only ten minutes to provision the average household for a month. The system worked best when there was only one item of each kind and one

•

•

standardised form of packaging. How such a system could have dealt with the 15,000 or more different items that previous generations had to cope with I don't know! So it was lucky that Compubuy was introduced at the same time as the politically astute government rationalised food manufacture, allowing only one product in each category – one sort of protein booster, one sort of vegetable concentrate, one sort of tea. It must have been confusing, to say the least, under a system where the same product masqueraded under half-a-dozen different names. The government benefited, too, by gaining an enormous pool of talent that previously had been employed upholding the myth of diversity and variety and difference between products.

'With Compubuy, each householder was allocated a specific ordering day – the same day for each residential agglomerate, and on that day the home computer would automatically start up. There was a catchy tune to remind people that it was shopping time, but I can't remember how it went ... On the screen would be a picture of the product, in its two or three different sizes, and the householder had only to touch the picture the required number of times. Three days later your order would be delivered. Of course, many products were irradiated for safe storage. The monthly box would be deposited in the well-insulated external pantry that was also accessible from the food preparation area, and whenever you wanted to make a meal you took the ingredients you needed and reconstituted them as necessary. If you didn't feel like doing this there was always the dish of the day prepared by the central kitchen of each tower of apartments. You simply reheated it, in its plastic sac. Any of the residents could buy some on the way home from work – though this wasn't exactly encouraged, and only a minimum number of serves was prepared each day.

●

●

As you can see, meal preparation required little skill, and as a result Professors of the Culinary Art were rare at this time. The only things people missed were frozen ices and creams – but then, these super-cows were designed to yield milk, not cream.

'In this era of ecological pragmatism, the vegetarian movement was very strong, and some of its members were prominent in government – in fact, I think they represented the remnant of those pesky Neo-Vegetarians who had persuaded the government of the twentieth century to legislate against the raising of animals for meat. They could usually count on the support of the biostatisticians and the Hippocratic Society, and although their arguments – that meat was unnatural, unhealthy and expensive – provoked much debate, politicians were too intimidated to oppose them. In any case, the majority party was controlled by the former beef barons who had invested their money elsewhere – in hydroponics.

'All fruits and vegetables were grown hydroponically, in vast, centrally located, glass-walled skyscrapers. The system was highly efficient, since there was no need to harvest the vegetables. The individual containers were simply transported to the Distribarn, and from there to the consumers. The external pantries all had a Growlight and the vegetables only needed a little water during the month. Households had vegetables at the peak of freshness, harvested to order when required. This was considered an enormous advance, and the credit must go to the vegetarians.

'After a while the novelty of Compubuy began to wear off, especially when instances of misuse occurred. I remember that in my niece's area, the program would sometimes come on in the afternoon, interrupting the children's homework session. It didn't matter until one afternoon she was late, and young Willy decided to play games. They ended up with 39 packets of Aminex, a dehydrated protein concentrate that you added to soups or to vegetable purees, and 24 cartons of sarsparilla tea. Still, I think people conceded that the system was efficient, and put up with it. From time to time there were underground grumblings about foods always tasting the same, or tasting of nothing, but people seemed to calm down and generally accepted what they were given. (There were rumours of suspicious substances having been added to the water supply or below-optimum iodine levels, but no one was able to prove anything.)

'But it was the water that eventually proved the downfall of this society. The Water Supply Board was dominated by vegetarians, because of their interest in the hydroponics industry, the largest user of water – although, to be fair, it also used recycled water. The milk reconstitution plants were only slightly less greedy. The gigapolis was on the coast, and most of this water was distilled from the sea by means of an ingenious energy-efficient system. As far as we can reconstruct the mechanism, it relied on an elaborate three-dimensional maze of electrically-charged semi-permeable membranes, after the sea water had been through a series of mechanical and enzymatic filters. The system worked perfectly well as long as the concentration of organic matter remained below a certain critical level.

'Looking back, it was unjust to blame the vegetarians for the final disaster. They had scientifically sited the distillation plants far off-shore, and piped the distilled water to land. According to their calculations the plants were far enough away from the old sewage outlets that still carried some waste into the ocean, and in any case the filtering devices had been designed to cope with the kind of

•

•

suspensions found around the outlets. No one knows whether the tides and the currents went awry at this time (astrologists suggested a disturbance in the upper stratosphere), or whether a new organism, smaller than any previously detected, was able to get through the filter system. In any case, distillation came to a standstill.

'Of course, people were not informed of the accident for a few days, and when the news was made public they were told that it was just a minor fault that could soon be rectified. Some started to get suspicious when their taps would sometimes stop running, and a few intrepid citizens began their own investigations. After that it was not long before the full effect of the calamity was realised, and the whole system of the society went into shock.

'I won't recount to you the horrors that went on the gigapolis. It was each to his own, and any theories of social responsibility were jettisoned in the struggle for survival. Those who didn't leave the gigapolis in the early days had no chance, and those who managed to escape needed enormous stamina and resourcefulness to stay alive. People had to work out what parts of what plants were edible, or how they could be made edible, and where to find safe water. Through careful experimentation they developed the knowledge that allowed them to survive and a diet that kept them healthy. Eventually groups of people came together in small communities, sharing the tasks of food production and preparation and teaching these skills to the children – for by this time there were children, too.

'The rest of the story is well known to all of you in the audience, the descendants of those 'went bush' and survived. You have inherited their courage, their wisdom, their inventiveness. Use them well.'

SIN AND WELL-CONSIDERED

INDULGENCE

*There is a fine line between the simple enjoyment of eating
and drinking, and eating and drinking simply for their
enjoyment — a line so fine that the moralisers feel
obliged to take out their indelible ink and rule it
heavy and black.*

GLUTTONY, AS REPRESENTED in a television series on the Seven
Deadly Sins, was a young woman who wanted it all, and wanted it
now – work, career, family, study. You would hardly call her greedy, in

●

●

the usual, piggish sense of greedy; she was simply a young woman whose appetites were unrestrained.

This is not the standard image of Gluttony, usually defined loosely as 'excess in eating'. However, back in the days when the Seven Deadly Sins were far more real than a few hours of television, what constituted Gluttony was solemnly spelled out. In essence, Gluttony meant 'excess in eating', but this was specifically itemised as eating too early in the morning, before prayers; eating too often (which meant more than two main meals a day); eating too quickly, swallowing foods without bothering to chew them; and eating too luxuriously. But these were only superficial slips compared with the real sin – disrespect towards God and the established order – that was often their corollary. Excess in eating might have been frowned on, but the consequences of over-eating or, more particularly, overdrinking were far more dangerous. The loss of self-control could lead to supplementary sins such as blasphemy and ribaldry (considered particularly shameful in a woman), absence from work or prayers because of a hangover, or other sins of which discretion usually forbade mention.

While the Church has cried out against gluttony, its representatives on earth have been the most consistent sinners. Balzac called gourmandism '*le péché des moines vertueux*', the pardonable sin of otherwise virtuous monks. Brillat-Savarin, too, recognised that monks, as a class, enjoyed their food (he may have called them gourmands, but never gluttons). 'If some men are predestined gourmands,' he wrote, 'others are gourmands by virtue of their calling; and mention must be made here of four great strongholds of gourmandism: finance, medicine, letters and religion.' The religious fraternities resisted some of the more obvious pleasures – dancing, gambling and the theatre –

•

•

but happily succumbed to the pleasures of eating and drinking. The fat friar, the plump and rosy-cheeked priest are caricatures, but they are drawn from real life.

Alphonse Daudet gives a sympathetic account of 'monkish gluttony' in his short story, *Les Trois Messes Basses*. Somewhere in rural Provence a country priest, dom Balaguère, is preparing to celebrate the three traditional Christmas Eve masses, to be followed by the midnight feast of *réveillon*. The priest has already seen the plump turkeys that will be the centrepiece of the meal, has watched the cook slipping thick black rounds of truffle between skin and breast, and can smell the tantalising aroma emanating from the kitchen of the château as he enters the chapel. What he doesn't recognise is the voice of the Devil, transformed into Garrigou the sacristan, whose little bell rings with increasing urgency, whispering, 'Hurry, hurry! The sooner you finish, the sooner you'll eat.' So the priest rushes through the masses, accelerating his delivery to the point that none of the congregation can keep up with him, and leaving out some prayers altogether, the more quickly to reach the festive table. There he drowns remorse for his sin with some good Châteauneuf wine ... only to be seized, a few hours later, by a terrible attack of indigestion, from which he dies without having had the opportunity to confess.

There's a parallel here with the story of Eve, who also yielded to the temptation of pleasure – the Devil that time cunningly camouflaged as a snake. For Gluttony was once the original and the first of the Seven Deadly Sins. By the fourteenth century it had been relegated to sixth on the list, and was represented as excess in eating and its consequences. But how do we get to Gluttony as 'excess in eating' from Gluttony as the prioritising of pleasure?

•

•

For poor dom Balaguère it was not overeating, or even over-drinking, that led to his ruin, but rather putting carnal appetite above spiritual obligation. There's the clue. It is only when the senses domi-nate and take control that gratifying the appetite becomes, if not a capital sin, at least a minor peccadillo – which is a fair indication of the way civilisation has privileged rationality. Indulgence, the gratifica-tion of desires, is not in itself to be condemned. Indulgence is simply doing something enjoyable and getting a thrill of pleasure from it. You can indulge an appetite for books – reading provides pleasure, know-ledge or amusement. The same motive takes you to the cinema. No one (except perhaps religious extremists) would frown on these plea-sures, because they're considered primarily intellectual. (Erotic books and films are an entirely different category.) Only when pleasures are seen as primarily sensual does suspicion creep in. Our civilisation is built on the premise that the intellect is superior to the senses, despite the fact that we are given senses for self-protection and to allow them to atrophy would be, at the very least, disrespectful. It's not the indulgence of desires that is necessarily reprehensible, but rather the immoderate indulgence of sensual appetite that occurs when reason is lost or thrown to the winds.

Gluttony, then, represented deviant behaviour. As such it threat-ened the equilibrium of society at the same time as it compromised the physical harmony of the body. In olden days, this constant menace was acknowledged and Gluttony was even licensed, on the one day each year given over to Carnival, as if this liberality would keep it in check for the rest of the year. Society would then function smoothly. Each individual would know his place and respect his duty, and desire would be subjugated to reason. The Church would retain hold of the reins.

•

•

It's as though the Church could not trust people to live the temperate life, to balance sensuality and rationality. Temperance – before it was corralled to serve the needs of the anti-alcohol campaigners – was honoured as a virtue. In both men and women, it was a quality to be esteemed. It represented Aristotle's Golden Mean, and assumed a considered appraisal of alternatives, a measured approach, an ideal of balance and harmony. It was the quality of *'mezura'* held high by courtly society in medieval Provence. *'Mas es fols qui.s desmezura'*, sang the troubadour Bernart de Ventadorn: foolish is he who does things out of measure.

Temperate, like Baby Bear's porridge, is 'just right' – though what is 'just right' depends, like ideas of taste, on the prevailing values of society. On the basis of their eating habits and table manners, the fourteenth-century Catalan philosopher Francesc Eiximenis awarded his compatriots the title of *'les pus temprats homens'*, the most temperate of men. Unlike other nationalities, he argued, they were content with just two dishes per meal, and to eat only two meals a day; they ate in the correct order, roast before boiled; and they carved their meat neatly, according to the prescribed manner for each – unlike the English, French, Germans and Italians who hacked at it indiscriminately. They sat at a table to eat, unlike the Castilians who sat on the floor; they wore their sleeves at a reasonable length, unlike the French and the Germans, whose long sleeves fell in the soup and unlike the immodest and bare-armed Castilians. Unlike the English and Germans who drank beer and mead and other curious beverages far removed from civilising wine, they drank the fermented juice of the grape, but not to excess as the French and Lombards did. Thus, he concluded, by these standards it was incontestably proven that the Catalans were

•

•

the most honest eaters, the most proper drinkers – indeed, the most temperate of men.

Eiximenis condoned indulgence – the simple gratification of appetites and desires – on the assumption that indulgence would be moderate and that pleasure was reasonable. The Church, on the other hand, took a severely pessimistic view – after all, it stood to lose. Indulgence, it believed, would inevitably be intemperate; the cycle of desire-pleasure-desire would become a maelstrom, sweeping up souls and spinning them directly to Hell. Once in its whorls, these souls would be out of control and beyond the Church's grasp. Fearing indulgence, the Church stamped on it, and hence its threats and maledictions, its regimentation of the various misdemeanours into a Capital Sin.

In the fifteenth century – about the same time as the spiritual authority of the Church began to be questioned – people started to speak out in favour of pleasure and what Brillat-Savarin later defined as gourmandism: the 'impassioned, reasoned and habitual preference for everything which gratifies the organ of taste'. 'What evil can there be in well-considered indulgence?' asked Bartolomeo Sacchi – biographer of the popes, librarian to the Vatican, and better known as Platina, author of *De Honesta Voluptate et Valitudine*. In his doctrine of *honesta voluptas*, which might roughly be translated as 'measured pleasures', Platina argued that there is pleasure to be had in eating and drinking (in moderation), that there is nothing shameful in the enjoyment of good food and wine, and that pleasurable eating is not incompatible with good health. Hardly a revolutionary proposal today – but in retrospect, it is easy to see why Platina felt the need to justify his ethic.

●

●

*I know full well that a number of unsympathetic persons will find fault
with me, saying that I wish to encourage a life of ease and pleasure.
But I speak to those who are so austere and full of pride and who voice
judgment not on the basis of the experience of pleasure but by the name
alone. What evil can there be in well-considered indulgence? For pleasure
and health are called the mean between good and evil . . . I speak of that
indulgence which is between the bounds of good living and of those things
which human nature seeks.*

Honest indulgence, the sort Platina encouraged, is neither evil
nor to be feared. Rather, it is to be acknowledged, approved, turned to
intelligent advantage. I do not hesitate to indulge my fondness for
figs. All figs – fresh and dried, especially the Smyrna figs on their thread
of straw. I love the small brown honey-sweet ones from scraggy,
stunted trees that take root in the most inhospitable places, seemingly surviving on fresh air alone, like some bird out of medieval
mythology. I love the pendulous, purple-black figs that split open to
reveal insides of raspberries-and-cream, the ones I watched and
patiently waited for, one summer in Provence.

But I would be a liar if I did not confess to having eaten, on occasion, a surfeit of figs – such that my tongue tingled, my mouth and
lips chafed, and still I would eat just one more. The balance between
enough and excess is a delicate one. There is a fine line between the
simple enjoyment of eating and drinking, and eating and drinking
simply for their enjoyment – a line so fine that the moralisers feel
obliged to take out their indelible ink and rule it heavy and black.

To counter the moralisers I would argue that the enjoyment of
food and drink is not just the gratuitous satisfaction of sensual

•

•

appetites – unless one is parched from thirst or ravenous with hunger. As Madame de Sévigné said about fresh green peas when they arrived at Versailles in the seventeenth century, there is the pleasure of antici-pation, the pleasure of eating them – and the pleasure of remembering this pleasure. The enjoyment of eating and drinking includes thinking about what and how one eats and drinks; it involves choice, and choice entails discrimination and judgment, reflecting on the food as you eat it and sending the sensations (suitably coded) to a mental data bank for future reference. And in turn, this means resort to language. Finding the right words to describe the cabernet swirling round your mouth, or the respective qualities of Victorian and Tasmanian bries, demands, in addition to a sensitive palate, a well-tuned and well-exercised mind.

But the spectre of sin, or at least of something not quite proper, looms over this intellectual corollary of eating and indulging. Talking, reading and writing about food and drink are all too often seen as frivolous. Reflecting on meals eaten, dishes cooked is considered pure hedonism. Perhaps this is a hangover from a straight-laced age which frowned on any discussion of food and regarded all pleasures associated with food and drink as verging on gluttony.

In a dualistic framework where substance or matter is opposed to ideas, food is automatically assigned to the side of substance. Substance is the lesser of the two. There is no doubting the assumed superiority of ideas, of thinking and philosophising. Even though food is the basis of life it is generally seen as less worthy of intellectual attention. In newspapers food articles are relegated to the back pages; Writers' Weeks relegate food writing to the end of the program. How can we learn to apply our senses with discrimination if these very

•

•

processes are deemed less valuable to our self-preservation than knowing how electricity works?

When he spoke of 'well-considered indulgence' Platina was encouraging people to reflect on their choice of food and drink. Surely any wrong lies in the transgression of this principle. Gluttony today is not mere 'excess in eating' or even 'extravagant indulgence', which are both quantitative concepts, but unconsidered, thoughtless indulgence of the appetite. Eating and drinking without consideration of others – such as taking more than your share. Or eating carelessly, without regard to the earth's resources. Or eating and drinking without heed of the headache and hangover that inevitably follow an excess. The great nineteenth-century French writers on gastronomy, Brillat-Savarin and Grimod de La Reynière, went to great length to distance gluttony from gourmandism, which they described as the enjoyment of eating without overeating (both would have been equally critical of 'swallowing foods without bothering to chew them'). Brillat-Savarin called gourmandism the enemy of excess, and saw indigestion and drunkenness as the real offences. Indeed, Grimod anticipated a gastronomic journal which would include reports on '*toutes les indigestions célèbres*' – a public black-listing of all of society's tired and emotional misjudgments – as if this would be mete punishment for intemperate indulgence.

It's time to rewrite the dictionary definition. More than immoderate, unrestrained appetites, Gluttony is the outward manifestation of not thinking and not caring about what goes into your mouth. Not thinking about what you want and need and how to balance and satisfy the two, not reflecting on the messages from the senses. Gluttony represents a disregard of flavour.

•

•

The American philosopher Henry Thoreau once wrote (anyone who can write so affectionately of loons over Walden Ponds deserves to be listened to) that the person who distinguishes the true savour of his food can never be a glutton, while the person who fails to do so cannot be otherwise. And in a way, this is the real sin – wolfing down the food, gulping the drink, without pausing to think or taste and silently give thanks.

BIBLIOGRAPHY

Abbott, Edward. *The English and Australian Cookery Book.* London: Sampson Low, 1864.

Adams, Francis. *The Australians: A Social Sketch.* London: T. Fisher Unwin, 1893.

Aron, Jean-Paul. *The Art of Eating in France: Manners and Menus in the Nineteenth Century.* New York: Harper & Row, 1975.

Atkinson, James. *An Account of Agriculture and Grazing in New South Wales.* London: J. Cross, 1826. 2nd ed, rev. London: J. Cross/Simpkin, Marshall & Co, 1844.

Barnard, Marjorie. 'Our Literature', in *Australian Writers Speak.* Sydney: Angus & Robertson, 1943.

Barnes, Agnes K, ed. *The CWA Cookery Book and Household Hints.* First publ. 1936. 2nd ed, rev. Perth: E.S.Wigg & Son, 1937.

Barthes, Roland. 'Towards a psycho-sociology of contemporary food consumption', in *Food and Drink in History.* Ed. R. Forster & O. Ranum. Baltimore: John Hopkins University Press, 1979.

Blainey, Geoffrey, ed. *Greater Britain: Charles Dilke visits her new lands, 1866 & 1867.* Sydney: Methuen Haynes, 1985.

Bocuse, Paul. *La Cuisine du Marché.* Paris: Flammarion, 1976.

Breton, Lieut. *Excursions in New South Wales.* 2nd ed, rev. London: Bentley, 1834. Facs. Johnson Reprint corporation, 1970.

Boulestin, Marcel & Laboureur, Suzanne. *Petits et Grands Plats.* Paris: Au Sans Pareil, 1928.

Brillat-Savarin, Jean-Anthelme. *Physiologie du Goût. (Physiology of Taste).* First publ. 1825. Trans. Anne Drayton, *The Philosopher in the Kitchen.* Harmondsworth, Middlesex: Penguin, 1970.

Calvino, Italo. *Mr Palomar.* Trans. William Weaver. London: Pan, 1986.

Carrier, Robert. *Great Dishes of the World.* London: Nelson, 1963.

Clarke, Marcus. *The Future Australian Race.* Melbourne: A.H. Massina and Co, 1877.

Clarke, Marcus. *A Colonial City.* Ed. L.T. Hergenhan. St. Lucia: University of Queensland Press, 1972.

Comettant, Oscar. *In the Land of Kangaroos and Gold Mines.* First publ. 1890. Trans. Judith Armstrong. Adelaide: Rigby, 1980.

Cookery Book of Good and Tried Receipts ('*The Presbyterian Cookery Book*'). First publ. 1895. 12th ed. Sydney: Angus & Robertson, 1912.

Daudet, Alphonse. 'Les Trois Messes Basses', in *Contes du Lundi.* First publ. 1873.

David, Elizabeth. *An Omelette and a Glass of Wine*. First publ. 1984. Harmondsworth, Middlesex: Penguin, 1986.

David, Elizabeth. *French Provincial Cooking*. First publ. 1960. Harmondsworth, Middlesex: Penguin, 1964.

David, Elizabeth. *Mediterranean Food*. First publ. 1950. Harmondsworth, Middlesex: Penguin, 1965.

Davidson, Alan & Davidson, Jane, trans. *Dumas on Food*. London: Michael Joseph, 1978.

Davidson, Alan. *Mediterranean Seafood*. Harmondsworth, Middlesex: Penguin, 1972.

Dawson, Robert. *The Present State of Australia*. London: Smith Elder and Co, 1830.

Doling, Annabel. *Vietnam on a Plate: A Culinary Journey*. Hong Kong: Roundhouse Publications (Asia), 1996.

Douglas, Norman. *Old Calabria*. First publ. 1915. Harmondsworth, Middlesex: Penguin, 1962.

Driver, Christopher. *The British at Table, 1940–1980*. London: Chatto & Windus, The Hogarth Press, 1983.

du Plessix Gray, Francine. *October Blood*. New York: Simon and Schuster, 1985.

Eiximenis, Francesc. *Com Usar Be de Beure e Menjar*. Introd. & ed. Jorge E. J. Gracia. Barcelona: Curial, 1977.

Eliot, T.S. *Notes Towards a Definition of Culture*. London: Faber & Faber, 1948.

First catch your kangaroo: A letter about food written from the Bendigo goldfields in 1853 by William Howitt to Eliza Acton. Adelaide: Libraries Board of South Australia, 1990.

Flannery, Tim. *The Future Eaters*. Melbourne: Reed Books, 1994.

Fowler, Frank. *Southern Lights and Shadows*. London: Sampson Row, 1859. Facs. Sydney: Sydney University Press, 1985.

Frye, Northrop. *Anatomy of Criticism*. Princeton: Princeton University Press, 1957.

Glasse, Hannah. *The Art of Cookery made Plain and Easy*. First publ. 1747. Facs. London: Prospect Books, 1983.

Grimod de La Reynière. *Almanach des Gourmands*. Paris: 1804.

Grogan D, Mercer C & Engwicht D. *The Cultural Planning Handbook: An Essential Australian Guide*. Sydney: Allen & Unwin, 1995.

Hackett, Lady, ed. *The Australian Household Guide*. Perth: E.S.Wigg & Son, 1916.

Halligan, Marion. 'The Marble Angel', in *The Living Hothouse*. St Lucia: UQP, 1988.

Hartley, Olga & Leyel, Mrs. *Lucullus: The Food of the Future*. London: Kegan Paul, 1927(?).

Horne, Donald. *The Public Culture: The Triumph of Industrialism*. London/Sydney: Pluto Press, 1986.

La Varenne. *Le Cuisinier François*. Paris: 1651.

Lake, Max. *Food on the Plate, Wine in the Glass, according to the workings and principles of Flavour*. Sydney: 1994.

●

●

Laubreaux, Alin. *The Happy Glutton*. Trans. Naomi Walford. London: Ivor Nicholson and Watson, 1931.

Leakey, Richard. *The Origin of Humankind*. First publ. 1994. London: Phoenix, 1995.

Lin, Hsiang Ju & Tsuifeng. *Chinese Gastronomy*. First publ. 1969. London: Jill Norman & Hobhouse, 1982.

Luce, Henry R. 'The challenge of the future: an overview', in *Food & Civilization: a symposium*. Washington DC: Charles C Thomas, 1966.

Maloney, Ted. *Cooking for Brides*. Sydney: Ure Smith, 1965.

Maclurcan, Mrs Hannah. *Mrs Maclurcan's Cookery Book: A Collection of Practical Recipes, Specially Suitable for Australia*. First publ. Townsville, 1898.

Malraux, André. *The Voices of Silence*. Trans. Stuart Gilbert. First publ. 1953. Frogmore, St Albans: Paladin, 1974.

Malouf, David. 'A Traveller's Tale', in *Antipodes*. London: Chatto & Windus, The Hogarth Press, 1985.

Marinetti, F.T. & Fillìa. *La Cuisine Futuriste*. Trans. Nathalie Heinich. Paris: Editions A–M Métailié, 1982.

Markham, Gervase. *The English Hus-wife*. London: 1615.

Marshall, Jock & Drysdale, Russell. *Journey among Men*. First publ. 1962. Melbourne: Sun Books, 1966.

Melville, Henry. *The Present State of Australia*. London: G.Willis, 1851.

Meredith, Louisa. *Tasmanian Friends and Foes*. Hobart Town/London: J Walch & Sons/Marcus Ward & Co, 1880.

Messisbugo, Christoforo di. *Banchetti, Composizione di vivande et apparecchio generale*. Ferrara, 1549.

Meudell, George. *The Pleasant Career of a Spendthrift*. London: George Routledge & Sons, 1929.

Millan, Amado. 'Identité collective et innovation alimentaire', in *Information sur les Sciences Sociales*: 1991. 30 (4): 739–755.

Monro, Amie. *The Practical Australian Cookery*. 2nd ed, rev. & enl. Sydney: Dymocks, 1909.

Moorhouse, Frank. *Days of Wine and Rage*. Melbourne: Penguin, 1980.

Mundy, Godfrey Charles. *Our Antipodes*. London: Bentley, 1862.

Muskett, Philip E. *The Art of Living in Australia*. London: Eyre and Spottiswoode, 1893. Facs. Sydney: Kangaroo Press, 1987.

National Research Council. *Designing Foods: Animal Product Options in the Marketplace*. Washington, DC: National Academy Press, 1988.

Pan, Hanna, ed. *Australian Hostess Cookbook*. Sydney/Melbourne: Nelson, n.d.

Petitot, M, ed. *Memoirs de Messire Olivier de la Marche*. Foucault: Paris, 1920.

Platina. *De Honesta Voluptate et Valitudine.* Trans. of 1475 Venice ed. by Elizabeth Andrews. St Louis: Mallinckrodt, 1967.

Porter, Hal. *The Watcher on the Cast-Iron Balcony.* London: Faber and Faber, 1963.

Presbyterian Cookery Book (Cookery Book of Good and Tried Receipts). First publ. 1895. 12th ed. Sydney: Angus & Robertson, 1912.

Rawson, Mrs L. *The Antipodean Cookery Book and Kitchen Companion.* First publ. 1895. Facs. Sydney: Kangaroo Press, 1992.

Revel, Jean-François. *Culture & Cuisine: A journey through the history of food.* Trans. Helen Lane. New York: Da Capo, 1984.

Reynolds, Cuyler. *The Banquet Book.* New York: G.P. Putnam's Sons, 1902.

Rifkin, Jeremy. *Beyond Beef: The rise and fall of the cattle culture.* Melbourne: Viking, 1992.

Ritchie, J. Ewing. *A Summer in Australia.* London: Fisher Unwin, 1890.

Root, Waverley. *The Food of France.* New York: Alfred A. Knopf, 1972.

Rozin, Elizabeth. *Ethnic Cuisine: the Flavor Principle Cookbook.* First publ. 1973. Lexington, Mass: S. Greene Press, 1983.

Rutledge, Mrs Forster. *The Goulburn Cookery Book.* First publ. 1899. 15th ed. Sydney: Edwards, Dunlop, 1913.

Scully, Terence, ed. 'Du fait de cuisine par Maistre Chiquart 1420', in *Vallesia*: 40. Sion: 1985.

Seed, Diane. *The Top One Hundred Pasta Sauces.* Sydney: Simon & Schuster, 1987.

Seed, Diane. *The Top One Hundred Italian Dishes.* Sydney: Simon & Schuster, 1991.

Sokolov, Raymond. *Fading Feast: A Compendium of Disappearing American Regional Foods.* First publ. 1979. New York: EP Dutton Inc, 1983.

Spencer, Colin. *The Heretic's Feast: A History of Vegetarianism.* London: Fourth Estate, 1993.

Stein, Gertrude. *The Autobiography of Alice B. Toklas.* London: John Lane, The Bodley Head, 1933.

Symons, Michael. *The Shared Table: Ideas for Australian Cuisine.* Canberra: AGPS, 1993.

The Barossa Cookery Book : Four Hundred Selected Recipes from a district celebrated throughout Australia for the excellence of its cookery. First publ. 1917. 2nd ed. Adelaide: Hunkin, Ellis & King, 1931.

The Kookaburra Cookery Book. First publ. 1911. 2nd ed. Melbourne: E.W.Cole, 1912.

The Satyricon of Petronius. Trans. Paul Dinnage. London: Spearman & Calder, 1953.

The Woman's Mirror Cookery Book. Sydney: the *Bulletin*, 1937.

Thomas, Dylan. *Under Milk Wood.* First publ. 1954.

Visser, Margaret. *Much Depends on Dinner.* New York: Macmillan, 1986.

Wilson, C. Anne. *Food and Drink in Britain, from the Stone Age to recent times.* London: Constable, 1973.

INDEX

WAKEFIELD PRESS

Kangaroo Cookin'

— ♫ —

88 simple roo recipes
Peter Winch, Andrew Thompson & Kent McCormack

Put some bounce in your kitchen
with the world's first kangaroo cookbook.
It's bound to keep you a hop ahead of the mob.

ISBN 1 86254 326 7   RRP $12.95

WAKEFIELD PRESS

The Original Mediterranean Cuisine

—————————————— ♫ ——————————————

Medieval recipes for today
Barbara Santich

'*The Original Mediterranean Cuisine* is a fascinating and intelligent book on a riveting subject. It is packed with gems of information and also provides delicious eating.'

CLAUDIA RODEN

Robust, gutsy flavours, sophisticated and subtly spiced sauces: this is the original Mediterranean cuisine.

Here is a book that brings authentic medieval food to today's table, with seventy recipes translated and adapted from fourteenth and fifteenth century Italian and Catalan manuscripts. Inside you will find such intriguing delights as ginger and almond sauce, chicken *mig-raust*, figs with rose petals and Platina's herb salad.

You will also learn the story of Mediterranean cuisine to the end of the fifteenth century, before tomatoes, potatoes and peppers arrived from the New World.

ISBN 1 86254 331 3   RRP $24.95

WAKEFIELD PRESS

Wakefield Press has been publishing good Australian books for over fifty years. For a catalogue of current and forthcoming titles, or to add your name to the mailing list, send your name and address to Wakefield Press, Box 2266 Kent Town, South Australia 5071

Telephone (08) 8362 8800   Fax (08) 8362 7592

Wakefield Press thanks Wirra Wirra Vineyards and the South Australian Department for the Arts and Cultural Development for their continued support.